Retaining Effective Teachers

Retaining Effective Teachers

A Guide for Hiring, Induction, and Support

Mary C. Clement

ROWMAN & LITTLEFIELD
Lanham • Boulder • New York • London

Published by Rowman & Littlefield
A wholly owned subsidiary of The Rowman & Littlefield Publishing Group, Inc.
4501 Forbes Boulevard, Suite 200, Lanham, Maryland 20706
www.rowman.com

Unit A, Whitacre Mews, 26-34 Stannary Street, London SE11 4AB

British Library Cataloguing in Publication Information Available

Library of Congress Cataloging-in-Publication Data

ISBN 978-1-4758-2837-5 (cloth : alk. paper) -- ISBN 978-1-4758-2838-2 (pbk. : alk. paper) -- ISBN 978-1-4758-2839-9 (electronic)

∞ ™ The paper used in this publication meets the minimum requirements of American National Standard for Information Sciences Permanence of Paper for Printed Library Materials, ANSI/NISO Z39.48-1992.

Printed in the United States of America

This book is dedicated to Mrs. Faye Snodgress, the Executive Director of Kappa Delta Pi, the international honor society in education. Faye is the single most supportive administrator with whom I have worked, and Kappa Delta Pi is my professional support network.

Contents

Preface

I was a high school foreign language teacher for eight years. I left traditional classroom teaching to earn my advanced degrees and become a professor of education. I often ask myself what would have kept me in the classroom, since I was the "highly qualified" teacher discussed in so much of the literature on teacher retention. Would a mentor or five-year induction program have led to my retention in that school?

Would a higher salary have kept me in the classroom? Perhaps I needed a career ladder where I could teach half a day and work as a professional developer the rest of the time. Would more positive support from the administration have been the answer?

In my eight years of teaching I only attended about four conferences, and those were half-day workshops at a nearby university. What if every two years I had been able to attend a national or international conference? Quite frankly, maybe I just wanted to work in an air-conditioned classroom that was actually large enough to accommodate the number of students enrolled in my classes.

As a professor of teacher education, my research has centered on the hiring of effective teachers for K–12 classrooms. Of course, like other researchers, I have learned that hiring is sometimes a revolving door, even when the best possible new teachers arrive at a school. While I believe that retention begins with hiring, the steps after hiring and throughout a teacher's career are crucial to long-term retention.

As the Millennial students (those born 1980 to 2000) entered colleges and teacher education programs, I began to read and learn about generational studies and about Generation Y—the Millennials. When I looked at the literature about Millennials in business workplaces, the comparisons to Millennials in the workplace of schools were recognizable. Millennial teachers have an array of experiences different from my generation's background.

These new teachers want quick, positive feedback often, and they probably won't just listen in a faculty meeting. They will push the envelope with their constant questions of "why." They want, and may demand, some supports for their work that previous generations of administrators never thought of providing. These supports may develop into improvements of the school as a workplace for all employees, not just the new teachers.

So, what will retain today's effective teachers in the profession? The combination of a workplace that meets or exceeds their expectations is one answer to this question. Proactive administrative support combined with collegial mentoring and extended induction programs contribute to retention.

Valid, clear evaluation procedures help to promote the growth of teachers and to make the determination of "effective." Creating teacher leader positions keeps teachers in classrooms and allows for professional growth. Advancement opportunities and leadership roles help to retain teachers while growing the next generation of administrators.

HOW TO USE THIS BOOK

This book serves as a resource for all who seek to improve the retention of effective teachers in their schools and districts. Personnel directors, district administrators, building-level administrators, and teachers should be involved in retention efforts. To paraphrase the proverb: it takes a village to retain and support classroom teachers.

The first chapter is a starting point for any school that does not have a usable faculty retention plan in place or that seeks to improve its current plan. Retention plans include, and supersede, hiring procedures, orientation sessions, and basic mentoring programs. A retention plan begins with recruitment and hiring of "best fit" candidates and then includes the topics of chapters four through ten.

The first two chapters provide the research background on why retention is so critical in today's schools, and also what today's new teachers expect in their jobs. The generational research on teachers guides the support systems that need to be in place for them.

The book makes an excellent study for long-term planning at the district level and is a good choice for teachers who will lead orientation, mentoring, and collegial observation initiatives. It uses an easy-to-read format with checklists and templates in the appendices. Much current research on the teaching workforce, retention, and the workplace of teachers is included in this book, along with practical checklists and guidelines.

For anyone with questions about how to hire, induct, retain, and create the next generation of teachers in a school, the answers are here, in a highly readable style with practical examples. It serves as an excellent resource for graduate students in educational leadership/administration programs, as the reference list is exhaustive. In essence, the research has been done for graduate students and administrators who seek to learn more on the topics presented.

As I read dozens of books and hundreds of articles on teacher retention to write this book, one thing became glaringly obvious to me. We know why teachers leave the profession and we know what support systems retain them in classrooms. The key is to implement the necessary practices to make retention a reality in more schools—not a chance happening or one-time model. This book is a must-read for new administrators and all who seek to retain the most effective teachers in their schools.

Acknowledgments

I wish to thank Dr. Tom Koerner for his continued support with my writing. Tom provides insight and just the right amount of editing for writers. He has been instrumental in publishing my work in a timely, professional manner.

Special thanks to Eppie Snider and all of my former students who have become administrators. These wonderful principals have kept in touch to teach me more about school administration.

Additionally, my thanks go to the administrators at Berry College where I teach. Providing release time for professors to do research is indeed critically important if we are to contribute to the knowledge base in our disciplines.

Chapter One

Creating a Retention Plan

Failing to plan is planning to fail.

—Anonymous

Schools seem to have a plan for everything from fire drills to lunchroom etiquette. The curriculum is mapped, the extracurricular activities are on a calendar, and every minute of the school day is scheduled bell to bell. Administrators carefully follow student enrollment numbers and keep the statistics on attendance and student graduation. There is a plan for hiring enough new teachers before the first day of school, and there is orientation for new hires so that they fit into the faculty. There may be a mentoring program for new teachers, and there will definitely be a plan for teacher evaluation.

What's missing? It is the extended new teacher induction that is often missing, as well as a crafted plan for long-term retention. Good teachers don't just "grow on trees," and retaining effective teachers must be a priority for high student achievement and a successful school environment. Where should a district start to create a system-wide retention plan? What should each individual school do to create a climate of retention? What can the teachers themselves do to support each other?

BEGIN WITH THE RESEARCH

Much more is known about the attrition of teachers than the phrase, "half leave after five years." Ingersoll's work on teacher retention has been extensive, and his findings indicate a trend that the teaching force is becoming "greener" (Ingersoll, Merrill, and Stuckey, 2014). "Greener" means large numbers of new hires who are recent college graduates, as well as older, but inexperienced, new teachers. Additionally, "early attrition has increased

1

among this growing number of beginners" (Ingersoll, Merrill, and Stuckey, 2014, p. 13).

Many researchers have indicated that the problem is not the shortage of new teachers entering the profession, but the "revolving door" syndrome where "too many teachers are leaving the profession after only a few years" (Brill and McCartney, 2008, p. 751).

The next question becomes, what are the effects on students if their teachers are continually young or inexperienced? Henry, Bastian, and Fortner (2011) found that "on average, teachers substantially increase their effectiveness between their first and second years of teaching" (p. 271). They also found that teachers who stay for at least five year display, "the highest upward developmental trajectory" (p. 275).

When discussing teachers, it can be helpful to further separate which teachers are referenced—elementary, middle, high school, special needs, or a specific high-needs field like STEM (science, technology, engineering, and mathematics) education. In a Public Agenda report, Rochkind and his colleagues (2007) found differences between middle and high school teachers compared to elementary school teachers with respect to their preparation and job frustrations. Overall, they found that middle and secondary teachers were "less likely to say they regard teaching as a long-term career choice" (p. 4). Why? "For example, nearly nine in ten high school teachers (88 percent) say that the most pressing problems facing high schools come from 'social problems and kids who misbehave' rather than academic issues" (Rochkind et al., p. 12).

DeAngelis and Presley (2011) found that "attrition rates tend to be significantly higher for certain teachers (e.g., teachers with stronger academic backgrounds; teachers of science and special education) and teachers in certain schools (e.g., urban schools; schools with higher percentages of minority, low-income, and/or low-performing students)" (p. 612).

Reasons to Leave, Reasons to Stay

Ask any teacher in the profession, or one who has left, about the stressors of teaching, and be prepared to hear a litany of issues. Ingersoll (as cited in Winans, 2005) stresses the "lack of faculty influence" over work issues such as the curriculum and discipline as a major factor "driving ever more teachers to quit the profession before retirement age" (p. 41). A lack of empowerment certainly affects teachers' feelings of efficacy in their jobs, as do other factors—everything from workplace issues and school setting to salaries.

In a 2008 meta-analysis, Borman and Dowling (2008) found the following:

1. Teachers in urban and suburban settings have slightly higher attrition than teachers from rural schools.
2. Attrition was higher from small schools.
3. Private schools experience higher teacher attrition rates than public schools.
4. Low administrative support heightens teacher attrition.
5. Low participation in a mentoring program increases attrition.
6. Limited opportunities for collaboration and a lack of school-based teacher networks raised attrition. (pp. 387–90)

Farber's research (2010) is quite specific about reasons that teachers leave the profession. She writes about standardized testing, unsafe schools, unrealistic expectations placed on teachers, bureaucracy, parents, and a general lack of respect as the reasons that teachers leave their work.

Simply put, it is tough to teach in many school settings. The stressors of dealing with today's students, accountability issues, lack of administrative or community support, and limited mentoring and collaborative activities all contribute to teacher attrition.

What keeps teachers in the profession, besides just the opposite factors of what makes them leave? Job security is a factor, as are health and retirement benefits. Salary is identified as a factor for keeping teachers in the profession (Inman and Marlow, 2004). It is known that teachers enter the profession because they love children or love their subject matter, and sometimes that desire to work with children and one's discipline is strong enough to keep teachers in their classrooms.

Linda Darling-Hammond (2003) has long argued that improved working conditions, effective teacher preparation, and early support for new hires are keys to retention. Wong and Wong (2012) cite professional development, collaboration, and fully developed induction plans as the factors for keeping effective teachers. Teachers have an overwhelming need to see their students succeed.

Providing an environment where teachers can experience success is a huge issue in teacher retention. Moore Johnson (2004) wrote, "The environment of the school ultimately mediates teachers' ability to find satisfaction in succeeding with students" and "supportive conditions for successful teaching can be found in schools that are often thought of as hard places to teach" (p. 90).

RETAINING TEACHERS IN HIGH-NEEDS FIELDS

Ask anyone who works in the field of teacher hiring about teacher shortages, and you will hear the same story. "We always need teachers in special education, math, and science." The American Association for Employment in Education (2015) reports annually on educator supply and demand and their findings indicate high demand for math, biology, chemistry, and Spanish. There is medium demand for physics, other science fields, and many of the special education fields. Of course, the supply and demand for teachers may vary from region to region of the United States, as well.

Regional demand for teachers can include the need for those who teach English as a second language. Those teachers with ESOL, ESL, or ELL certification can be in high demand in some areas, but not in others. The high need for male teachers in elementary schools, and minority teachers throughout the United States, remains a constant concern.

When creating a retention plan, special attention may be given to retaining minority hires. All of the general suggestions apply to the retention of targeted populations, but additional supports may be needed. Can a focus group of current minority teachers be used to provide insight into the needs of newly hired minority teachers? Can minority teachers have access to minority mentors within, or outside of, the district? Brainstorming and then creating an action plan for retention of all teachers is needed.

What Defines Effective Teachers?

Throughout this book, the phrase "effective teachers" is used. Just what defines an effective teacher? Some administrators still repeat the old phrase regarding effectiveness, "I can't really define it, but I know it when I see it." Many researchers have written on the topic, usually outlining traits and characteristics of those who are effective.

McEwan's (2002) research defines effective teachers as ones who possess personal traits, teaching traits, and intellectual traits that make them effective. Her list includes passion, leadership, with-it-ness, instructional effectiveness, book learning, and street smarts (McEwan, 2002).

Stronge, Tucker, and Hindman (2004) researched qualities of effective teachers, summarizing those qualities as the ability to manage and organize a classroom, ability to implement instruction, and ability to monitor student progress. They include personal characteristics of a teacher on their effectiveness list. These personal characteristics include the teacher's sense of caring, fairness, and respect, as well as their attitude and ability to reflect on their practice.

Other research on effective teachers, such as that by Stronge (2010) and Danielson and McGreal (2000), has been focused on the evaluation aspect of M M M M M good" teachers. Stronge, Tucker, and Hindman (2004) maintain that the qualities of effective teachers can, and should, be used in both the hiring and evaluation processes.

Every school has evaluation systems in place. Evaluations should be designed to determine which teachers are effective and also to support effectiveness and retention. See chapter 7 on teacher evaluation for more information on this topic.

If the premise of the importance of qualified, effective teachers is accepted, how do we ensure that schools are fully staffed by such teachers? What defines an effective teacher within an effective school? Owings and Kaplan (2008) state the correlates of effective schools, as defined by the *Journal for Effective Schools*, including focused mission, orderly environment, commitment to high expectations, instructional leadership, opportunity to learn, monitoring of student progress, and communication. Hence, an effective teacher should be able to focus on the mission, maintain an orderly environment, commit to high expectations, and fulfill the other correlates at the classroom level. With strategic interviewing, it can be determined if teachers have the knowledge and skills to be effective when hired.

Marzano has produced much research on effective schools and effective teaching, including having a model of effective teaching. The Marzano (2012) model of effective teaching includes establishing and communicating learning goals, tracking student progress, maintaining classroom procedures, organizing lessons that address content, and having students practice and deepen their understanding of new knowledge.

If so much research has been generated on the topics of teacher attrition, retention, and effectiveness, with a well-developed knowledge base on how to stem the tide of those who leave the profession, why isn't more being done to retain successful teachers? The simplest answers are time and money. Establishing mentoring programs and providing high-quality professional development take time and a significant budget. Historically, teachers have been isolated in their classroom, and traditional evaluation has caused teachers not to seek help, for fear of termination.

A SYSTEM-WIDE RETENTION PLAN

A district plan results from looking at the research base and internal data before deciding where to go. It is important for the district to know its current retention numbers and to ascertain if the leavers are leaving for jobs in other schools or leaving the profession. The human resources department can supply this information or start tracking the data.

Once district-wide information is available, then look at individual school data. Are more high school teachers leaving, and if so, why? Do individual schools have difficulty retaining special education teachers; math, science, or minority teachers? Combining the district and school pictures will provide insight into developing a retention plan.

Using the data, determine the goals for the retention plan and write them out. Make them widely known to current teachers and administrators and ask for input. Can the local teachers' association/union be of help in determining final goals? With broad goals established, practices that are already in place can then be updated and improved. For example:

Goal: Use hiring practices that promote retention.
Question: What are we already doing that works?

Goal: Make orientation a time for work, but also a time to treat new hires like VIPs.
Question: Can a principal share what s/he does to make new hires feel special?

Goal: Use practicing teachers in the efforts to retain new teachers.
Questions: How can teachers who demonstrate best practice share their work? Can more teachers be involved in mentoring programs?

Goal: Increase retention by X percent.
Question: Who will track the data and how will it be shared?

Goal: Provide professional development opportunities over the first five years of hiring.
Questions: How can we find the time for continued professional development? What will be the costs?

By outlining the goals and questions, the group in charge of the plan can develop the retention plan and the time and budget needs. Use each chapter of this book as a resource for ideas and model plans. Allow ample time for brainstorming and formulating the plan. Be sure documentation is complete, as school personnel change very quickly.

The district retention plan is the umbrella for all of the schools, but much work is needed at the building level for retention. Determine which pieces of the retention plan must be at the school level. School-level issues may include class size, location of classroom for proper heat, cooling, and ventilation, relationships with colleagues, and overall relationships with the building administrators. As one human resource director quipped, "Often, the reason people leave any job, including teaching, is that they just can't get along with their boss."

Teachers can't be retained in a situation where they perceive no positive support from their immediate boss. They often don't stay when they perceive themselves to be working harder than their colleagues, yet receiving less support or fewer rewards. Administrators play a key role in the retention of teachers. When planning for retention, the training and supervision of those who lead the schools are important.

Thinking Outside of the Box

As one human resources employee stated, "We retain teachers with two things—cash and culture." More and more districts recruit by advertising not only salaries, but also by providing a dollar value listing of what their health and retirement benefits include. Stressing maternity and paternity leaves, health benefits, and early retirement packages can make a difference to candidates.

Some districts are forging collaborations with their local chambers of commerce and realtors to provide more community help to teachers. It may become more common for districts to provide help in finding housing, or providing low-interest loans for that housing. When teachers become involved community members they are also more likely to stay in their school.

The time has come for creative thinking about teacher retention. As district and building administrators create their retention blueprints, consideration can be given to including community leaders in the planning. If it takes a village to raise a child, it may also take a community to retain the most effective teachers in a school district.

Questions to Start Discussion of a Retention Plan

1. What are our goals for retention?
2. Where is the greatest retention need in our district? (Math and science? Minority candidates? Special ed?)
3. Do we know our current retention numbers?
4. Do we know where our leavers go? (Leave teaching? Go to another district?)
5. How can our hiring practices promote retention?
6. What does our current orientation look like and what needs improvement?
7. What do we do for new hires after orientation? Throughout the first two years?
8. What role can other teachers play in retention initiatives?
9. What workplace issues may be unresolved or need examination in our district's schools?
10. Do we offer professional development that encourages teachers to take leadership roles and remain in their classrooms? What more could we do?
11. Do we offer professional development to grow our own administrators?

12. What collaborative efforts might we pursue with colleges to help with retention?

13. With whom does the leadership rest for creating and sustaining our retention plan?

14. What are some budgetary considerations? Can any grant funding be secured for initiatives?

SUMMARY POINTS FOR SUCCESS

1. When developing or improving a blueprint for teacher retention, use as much of the research available that has been written.

2. Consider the generational research on who is entering the teaching force and what they seek in their jobs.

3. The district needs an umbrella plan for retention and each school can develop local guidelines for support.

4. Work on teacher retention takes place year-round and needs a director, or an administrative leader and a steering committee.

5. Involve teachers in the process. Ask them what they seek and need to continue in their classrooms.

Chapter Two

This Generation of Teachers

This is a portrait of a generation on a tightrope.

—Levine and Dean (2012, p. ix)

Just as new teachers lament that today's students are so different from when they were in school, so too are administrators finding that their new hires are a different generation of teachers. Today's new teachers *are* of a different generation. They are the Millennials, born between 1980 and 1999 (Sujansky and Ferri-Reed, 2009). Also called Generation Y by some researchers (Rebore and Walmsley, 2010), they are most famous for being called the "Me Generation" (Twenge, 2006).

GENERATIONAL RESEARCH

Much was written when the Millennials went to college, as college professors struggled to understand the mindset of their students. In general, these students grew up in protected environments, being shuttled from one activity to the next, winning trophies for participation, and being told that they were always special. College professors have been exhorted to change their teaching strategies to meet the needs of their Millennial students.

Since Millennial college students want a rationale for what they are asked to do, professors who provide the "why" for their lectures and assignments get much higher course evaluations. These students want their instructors to know who they are, understand their issues, and make their instruction personalized on a daily basis. They also want to attend class on their timetable, with lectures and assignments available through technology to meet their busy schedules.

Millennials are further characterized as being "digital natives" and the busiest multitaskers ever. In class, students feel that they can text while listening to a lecture or viewing a video clip chosen by the professor. Levine and Dean (2012) wrote, "In contrast to their predecessors, today's college students are more immature, dependent, coddled, and entitled" (p. xiii). College students really do ask questions like, "Is the due date firm, or just a recommendation, and why?" Fast-forward to the world of work, and now this generation makes up almost a third of the workforce.

As the Millennials have entered the workplace, books like *Keeping the Millennials* (Sujansky and Ferri-Reed, 2009), *Managing the Millennials* (Espinoza, Ukleja, and Rusch, 2010), and *Becoming the Boss* (Pollack, 2014) have hit the bookshelves. What do Millennial employees seek in their workplaces? According to Sujansky and Ferri-Reed, they seek:

1. work-life balance;
2. career paths that include quick promotions and growth;
3. the latest technology;
4. quick, positive feedback;
5. a "cool" corporate culture;
6. to be appreciated;
7. to be challenged;
8. to be mentored;
9. to receive advancements;
10. to work in positive environments;
11. to have fun at work;
12. to learn in short, hands-on, real situations.

Obviously, some of the expectations listed above are diametrically opposed to school as a workplace. Classroom teachers do not earn advancements quickly, nor do they feel appreciated by their communities and our culture. Many schools do not meet the definition of being "cool" work environments or fun places to work. With this in mind, the difficulties of reconciling school as a workplace, with Millennials' expectations may be decidedly challenging.

Advice to those who manage the Millennials in the workplace has focused on adaptability and the confidence of managers to allow their twenty-something employees to challenge them. Managers who are challenged on their "ideas, processes, and ways of doing things" tend to be more effective than those managers who feel they should actually sanction or punish a challenge from employees (Espinoza, Ulkeja, and Rusch, 2010, p. 26).

Seeing young employees as a key to success in the workplace, rather than an impediment, is critical for a manager of Millennial employees. Pollack (2014) wrote that listening is a key to managing in today's world of work.

"The worst thing you can do is hide in your office; you have to go out and spend time with the troops" (p. 171).

Some limited research exists on Millennial teachers in the workplace. Howe and Strauss (2008) found that this generation of teachers has the following attitudes:

1. They expect to be treated as VIPs.
2. They assume they are protected.
3. They have long-term goals.
4. They thrive with structure and feedback.
5. They work best in teams and want to help their community.

What are the takeaway lessons learned from the knowledge base of generational research? Can administrators refine their hiring, induction, and long-term retention plans to meet the needs of Millennial generation teachers? And, if so, what supports are needed to keep this generation of teachers in K–12 classrooms?

What Millennial Teachers Seek

Most who work in education have heard the common laments of teachers who leave the profession. "It was just not at ALL what I expected." "The students were so needy, and I had to be the parent, the teacher, and their personal counselor." "The accountability for test scores drove me crazy." "Having to differentiate lessons for special education students, English language learners, and talented students in one room was just too much." "My principal had no idea what I was going through, and wasn't there to offer support, but just to criticize." "The old guard of teachers were counting the days to retirement and weren't there to help the new hires." "The testing schedule is crazy and I am becoming a teacher who just does test prep." What has to change to keep teachers in classrooms?

By comparing the literature on the Millennial generation to the issues of hiring, induction, and long-term retention of teachers, comparisons can be made. Change slow hiring communication to include quick, almost instant e-mail messages about receipt of materials. Think about Amazon's amazingly instantaneous communication about an order. This is what Millennials expect. While communicating during the hiring process, woo candidates. Appeal to their sense of specialness.

Make orientation and induction activities "cool" with group and bonding activities. Follow-up with long-term induction programs. While supervision and evaluation are absolute musts to determine teacher effectiveness, include quick, positive feedback whenever possible. Today's new hires seek positive reinforcement—remember they used to get trophies for showing up!

Millennial hires want to be able to ask why, and to do so in a safe, protected environment. Imagine for a moment that a new hire asks the following in a faculty meeting: "Why are we doing that if a support person/ secretary can?" A principal might feel that his/her authority is being questioned and berate the teacher for such an audacious question. The new hire feels that he or she should be rewarded for thinking about the issue and asking this question. The difference in the mindset of each person is miles apart. A savvy principal recognizes the difference between a teacher seeking to understand rationale and one who is criticizing the boss.

Workplace issues in schools have long been an issue for teacher retention. Teachers don't have personal secretaries, office space, and schedules conducive to collegial conversations. Teachers often remain isolated in their work. The Millennials will want to connect, both in person and through technology. Making both time and technology available will be important in their retention.

The sense of working on one's own timetable is important to Millennials. They feel that they should be able to plan lessons on their tablets while sipping coffee in Starbucks, and shouldn't have to sit in their classrooms to do so. (Simple, yet expensive, solution: Put a Starbucks-style café in the school with big tables for working. I have seen it done in schools with high teacher morale.)

In a 2015 movie, *The Intern*, a seventy-year-old character portrayed by Robert De Niro works in an office of twenty-something Millennials. He learns a lot from his young boss, who eventually comes to respect him greatly. The other employees learn a multitude of life lessons from him. It was the open-mindedness of both the seventy-year-old and the twenty-somethings that made the situation work splendidly. Of course, there were bumps along the way, and it took time for the twenty-somethings to learn how to listen to De Niro's character. Maybe just reinforcing listening, patience, and acceptance of each other are keys to success in working with, and retaining, Millennial teachers.

Being explicit and diplomatic at the same time is a skill. When working with Millennial employees, or all employees, diplomacy is important. However, all employees must do certain tasks and must present themselves professionally. Orientation about matters that are non-negotiable is important, and presenting non-negotiable issues with a rationale will work best with Millennials.

Consider the following scenario: A newly hired teacher attends his/her first parent discipline conference dressed casually and wearing a nose ring. The senior administrator at the meeting is appalled, but the conference is completed. After the conference the senior administrator asks an assistant principal to address the dress code and professionalism with the teacher.

Remember that a new employee may be expecting high praise for staying after school and spending several hours preparing for the parent conference. His/her mindset is ready for congratulations and not a lecture on appearance. What could have been done to address the issue *before* the conference?

Millennials want a rationale, so the conference should be about rationale, and should definitely start, and end, with praise and congratulations. Be prepared for the employee to provide feedback about how the administration should have prepared teachers better for the situation.

If an administrator does not understand why new hires are seemingly complaining or sarcastic about any guidelines, form a short-term committee or discussion group of those hires and ask for input. Listen and then provide the rationale behind the meetings and guidelines for procedures. Of course, some of the suggestions received may seem outlandish or simply not doable, but listening and opening the conversation can be very productive. Focus on one or two changes that are doable and suggested by the teachers. Teachers seek input and teacher leadership.

A conversational meeting, or a session to air concerns, can be very productive, but needs guidelines. Consider the following:

1. Why is the meeting needed? How much time is allotted? Where and when can the meeting be scheduled?
2. Who is invited to attend? Will minutes be taken? With whom will the minutes be shared? Are there professional association/union issues to be considered for such a meeting?
3. Make a very clear agenda and stick to it. Have discussion items and action items.
4. Who will lead the meeting? Will the professional association/union have a representative there in addition to new teachers invited?
5. What are the outcomes of the meetings? How will they be shared? Will there be future meetings? Will a standing committee be established?

Sample agenda items:

1. Introductions of all at the meeting
2. Rationale of why the meeting was called
3. How the meeting will be conducted
4. Discussion of issue one
5. Discussion of issue two, three, and so forth
6. Conclusion and summary of actions or timeline

What Millennials seek in the workplace may not be that different than what all teachers seek in their work. Scherer (2012) posed the following question to noted educator Linda Darling-Hammond in an interview: "Schools and education leaders can't always change the policies affecting teachers, but what might they do to support their teachers?" (p. 23). Darling-Hammond's response included the following:

> Teachers want to be in environments where they are going to be successful with students, where they're getting help to do that, where they have good colleagues, where they're working as a team. Teachers, especially those just entering the profession, are generally collaboratively oriented people.
>
> What great schools, great principals, and great school teams know is that you support teachers by structuring group collaboration for planning curriculum, by building professional learning communities, by encouraging ongoing inquiry into practice. (Scherer, 2012, p. 23)

SUMMARY POINTS FOR SUCCESS

1. Today's new teachers are from a different generation than most of today's administrators.
2. Knowing the research base on Millennial employees, and looking at what the business world has learned about hiring and managing Millennials is valuable.
3. New hires from the Millennial generation seek feedback that is frequent and positive. They want to make a difference and be recognized for their work.
4. Communication is a key to working with all teachers, especially new hires of this generation.
5. Consider explaining the rationale behind why things are done the way they are done to ensure that Millennials understand the context of meetings, procedures, and rules.

Chapter Three

Retention Begins with Hiring

I felt like a won the lottery when the boss called and hired me.
—Anonymous new employee

A college recruiter once said that it is not enough to simply bring in new students, but rather his job should be to recruit new alumni. To make the point clearer, a new student can drop out of college quickly, not making it to graduation, just as a newly hired teacher can leave the classroom quickly. The key is to recruit and hire those effective teachers who will remain in their jobs and serve their students well.

Do you remember receiving your first job offer for a full-time teaching position? Many of us literally jumped up and down. Did you ever take a job and feel less than excited? Which scenario causes the new hire to stay in a position and which one causes the person to say, "I'll take it, but only until something better comes along?" Getting hired should feel exciting, and at the same time, the entire hiring process should be a recruitment tool that makes each new teacher feel appreciated. The sense of being valued in the workplace cannot be underrated, and today's new teachers want to feel a sense of belonging and appreciation before they are even hired.

THE HIRING PLAN

Recruiting and hiring teachers is a year-round job. The most effective districts start with their philosophy of striving to hire the very best teachers. These districts have a plan. These plans are used consistently and updated frequently. Plans include strategic advertising, recruitment, use of multiple interviews, and evaluation of each hiring season. Data-informed decision making about hiring and retention directs the process.

The district recruitment and hiring blueprint includes who is in charge of documenting, sharing, and updating of the plan. Human resources personnel, administrators, teachers, and new hires should all have input. The plan has work to be done each season of the year. To have the best data for decision making, a recruitment and hiring plan needs to include when to survey those who interview and those who have been hired recently.

District Recruitment and Hiring Plan

1. Who is in charge of documenting, sharing, and updating the plan?
2. How should it be created? (Consider using human resources personnel, administrators, teachers, and recent new hires.)
3. Fall: When a hiring season ends, survey new employees about their hiring experience. (Consider doing this at least every few years.)
4. Fall: Begin training all who will be involved in the next hiring season.
5. Fall: Set the dates for attending job fairs, hosting an in-house fair, and looking at potential open positions.
6. Winter: Attend and recruit at job fairs.
7. Winter: Build a pool of applicants.
8. Spring: During this traditional hiring season, set dates for on-site interviews.
9. Spring: Make use of teachers in the hiring process before the school year ends.
10. Spring: Finalize position openings.
11. Summer: Make any additional hires.
12. Summer: Keep new hires informed with clear communication from the central office, building-level administrators, and mentor teachers.
13. Summer: Plan for new teacher orientation, meetings with mentors, and induction programming.
14. Summer: Survey all who did the hiring for suggestions for improvement of the process.
15. Start the school year!

Administrators and teachers are extremely busy people, making it difficult to add recruitment and planning to their already full schedules. However, as soon as a new cohort of hires is complete one must start evaluating the hiring season and prepare for the next one. Training all who hire is critically important, as is surveying the new hires and building the orientation and induction programs.

While every school district's process for hiring may vary, it is important that the process be formalized. There should be a written hiring process document that outlines the following:

1. Who determines the openings and how are they advertised?
2. How is the teachers' union involved in hiring and what procedures must be in place to meet contractual agreements regarding advertisement of jobs and hiring?
3. If a central office coordinates application paperwork, how do the appropriate applications get to the local schools?
4. If teachers are involved in hiring, as committee members, or as department or grade-level chairs, what is their specific role with regard to final hiring decisions?
5. How are final decisions made?

The steps in the hiring process need to be clear for all involved. The best way to clarify the work is to include a flowchart or step-by-step guidelines in the written material and to teach the material as needed to all who are new to hiring.

Writing Job Advertisements

The job advertisement is a recruitment and retention tool not to be overlooked. Truth in advertising is not only a must, but is also the beginning of the new teacher's job expectations. By including as much information about each job as possible, a candidate should be able to decide if he/she is indeed a match for the job.

It does not take a research study to predict that teachers who leave during the first year, or early in their career in a school, may say, "This was not at all what I expected." Details about school demographics, test results, special student and faculty programs, and the district salary and benefits should be available in the advertisement or easily accessible with an online link.

A good job advertisement is "information rich." That means that as much information as possible is shared in the advertisement for the opening. When possible, make each advertisement as specific as possible with regard to subject and grade level. Since the majority of all candidates are only searching online, the district website must be user-friendly and information rich.

The quest for making the match of teacher to position may begin with the wording of the job advertisement. An advertisement should include as much information as is known about a position to net the widest pool of applicants with the background and skills needed (Clement, 2012). Advertising for "a third-grade teacher" is not nearly enough information.

An information-rich advertisement includes specific skills and expectations of a job opening. For example, if the demographics of the students to be taught include special education students and English language learners, that should be stated in the job position. Sorting the paperwork is much easier when administrators and their assistants know exactly which criteria to sort for as applications arrive. For example:

> City School District seeks candidates for three early education positions, K–4. Applicants must be fully certified with a state 04 teaching certificate. Hires will be expected to work in classrooms with inclusion students and English language learners. Preference given to candidates who have demonstrated an ability to raise student achievement and who are experienced in the *Read Always* program and with working with at-risk learners.

It is always a good idea to include a disclaimer about which schools the openings are at, as teachers work for districts and not individual schools. If several openings exist, clarify that a certain number of teachers will be hired and assignments made as staffing and enrollment needs are determined.

The use of online job advertisements has grown exponentially. Sites like teachers-teachers.com and schoolspring.com are quite common. The site diversityrecruitmentpartners.com assists school districts to recruit minority candidates. Every state has its own website for advertising openings. Some district administrators search LinkedIn for possible candidates for high-needs fields.

Traditional job fairs at colleges add to the ways to recruit. Consider sending both building-level administrators and teachers to college job fairs, but only after they have been trained in what to do at a fair. It can be a waste of time and money to just send people to a fair and say, "meet a few candidates and gather resumes."

Preparing to Attend a College Job Fair

1. What are the times available for our representatives to set up and meet candidates?
2. Is time slotted for individual interviews with candidates after initial meetings?
3. How will the room be arranged? Will there be privacy?
4. What will we distribute at the job fair? (Brochures about the district? List of openings? Salary schedule? Freebies?)
5. What will we bring to advertise? (Professionally made posters? Video clips on a screen?)
6. How will we screen applicants to make some decisions about those with whom we want to follow up?
   What will our basic questions be?

   - Tell about your best teaching experience.
   - What is your interest in our district?

- Describe the most important part of your teacher education program.
- What has been your best success with an individual student?
- What has been your biggest challenge and why?

7. How will we use the contacts made at the job fair to further recruit the potential new hires?
8. Evaluate the job fair for its value to the district with regard to candidate quality and cost effectiveness.

What's Different about Hiring Millennials?

An October 2015 *Fortune* article about hiring candidates within twenty-four hours of on-site interviews affirmed a company's commitment to the new hires and raised the employees' sense of connection to the company (Lewis, 2015). Of course, the candidates' qualifications were reviewed extensively before the job fair interviews, but it was the almost-instant job offer that initially "wooed" and "wowed" new employees.

Positive onboarding experiences added to the support of those hired, and a commitment of the company to create a positive workplace culture further helped new hires to be retained. Schools may have something to learn from this business example.

Timing is everything to some candidates. They read a job advertisement, submit their application online, and they want an instant response. They feel confident that they are fully qualified and sure that their credentials will wow the employer. When some materials are received, send an e-mail noting that, and resend an automatic e-mail when all materials are received. Providing candidates with a time frame for interviews and decision making helps them to feel that they are under consideration. Hearing nothing back for weeks simply does not fit their time mindset.

Think about what amazon.com does for customers. After an order is placed, the customer receives an e-mail and they receive another when the order has shipped. A customer can go back into their password-protected account and check on each order, as well. This is the expectation of the applicant for a position in a school. Failure to have this type of instant communication may send a message to the candidate that the school is not using current technology, or that they are not a viable candidate. First impressions matter a lot to candidates.

While it can be argued that Millennial employees seek what others have sought in the past, this generation of new employees, as teachers, does want a clear hiring timeline, quick communication, and the sense of wooing. What else can help? Follow-up messages from the time of hiring until new teacher orientation starts is important. Administrators can conduct interviews from the point of view of recruitment, and should remember that the strongest candidates are also deciding where and for whom they want to work.

Savvy candidates have been trained to interview their potential new bosses while being interviewed themselves. While employers strive to find out in a preliminary interview if candidates should merit on-site interviews, candidates are deciding if they want to pursue the next interview. The use of FaceTime, Skype, phone interviews, and job fair interviews can save much time and effort on the part of recruiters. Be sure that all who conduct these interviews are aware of how to interview, using behavior-based interview style questions to ascertain previous knowledge and experience.

Sorting Candidates from Application Materials

A list of specific criteria can be pulled from the job advertisement and should be written up as a checklist for sorting applications. The criteria may include receipt of all letters of recommendation and of required background checks. Any applications that are not complete or do not have evidence of meeting the stated criteria should not be considered.

Using a behavior-based approach, candidates who fail to submit all parts of the application will probably become teachers who fail to turn in all paperwork. (Past behavior is the best predictor of future performance.) Applicants with late paperwork will most likely have late paperwork when they are on the job. A careful sort of paperwork will narrow the number of applications to be forwarded to an administrator.

Once the basic sort of applications is completed, consider narrowing candidates by reading resumes, cover letters, and letters of recommendation. Create a checklist, criteria sheet, or rubric for doing this. Using three categories of "unacceptable," "acceptable," and "target" is one way to evaluate with more objectivity. Some choose to make a scale of 1 to 5 for evaluating the paperwork. Look for evidence of your predetermined criteria, making written notes and ratings on the evaluation instrument.

Cover letter:
Correct spelling, grammar, and punctuation in the cover letter
Clearly stated information about knowledge of school district
Overall good presentation in a short, one-page letter
A legible signature

Resume:
Easy to read
Correct spelling, grammar, and punctuation
Certification matches job
Experience matches job
Evidence of leadership and/or awards

Evidence of ongoing professional development

Letters of recommendation:
Writers recommend the candidate
Special strengths of the candidate are discussed
Writers saw the candidate teach

Application:
All sections completed
Submitted on time
Indicates appropriate experience
Rating of the original response questions
Legible handwriting on required hand-written section

BEHAVIOR-BASED INTERVIEWING

Behavior-based interviewing (BBI) is a style of interviewing that is built on the premise that past behavior is the best predictor of future performance (Fitzwater, 2000). Before the interview, the employer determines the past behaviors, experiences, and expertise needed by a candidate to do the job. Next, questions are developed to address those competencies.

BBI-style questions begin with stems that require a candidate to describe past work and success. These stems include: How have you . . . ? What has been your approach to . . . ? Describe how you have . . . . And tell me about a time when . . . . After the stem, the rest of the question is formed with a concrete topic needed for the job. In education, those topic areas are curriculum, standards, planning, management, assessment, parent communication, and differentiation of instruction. Specialized fields, such as art, music, physical education, and special education will have a distinct set of questions.

The use of behavior-based questions for all levels of interviews will increase the probability of hiring an effective new teacher. BBI can be applied to all steps of the hiring process. A candidate whose paperwork has spelling or grammatical errors will be a teacher whose work has similar errors. When a teacher cries in an interview, apologizing for the tears due to stress, he/she will also be the teacher who cries in front of students due to stress.

How does the preliminary interview provide the employer with what they need to know and provide expectations of the "woo" factor at the same time? Phrasing of the questions is one way. Examples might include the following:

1. We have an outstanding record at our school for increasing reading time in the upper elementary grades. Tell me about your experiences teaching reading in an upper elementary grade.

2. Our teachers receive common planning time for creating standards-based units and for determining how much time is needed for each unit. How have you approached long-term planning in the past? Describe how your teaching planning has been guided by standards.
3. Time is allotted at our school for teachers to observe other teachers for specific lesson ideas. What have you learned from being observed and from observing a cooperating teacher with whom you worked?

These questions start with a positive remark about the school and/or teachers' work, and then ask the candidate to explain his/her experience with the topic. In a short, twenty-minute preliminary interview, these positive remarks help the candidate get a better picture of the school and its support of teachers' work. (See appendix 3.1 for a preliminary interview checklist.)

Because of the ever-increasing cost of travel and because of the huge numbers of unqualified applicants who seek positions, preliminary interviews have become more important than ever. Preliminary interviews may take place at job fairs, by telephone, or over the Internet with Skype or other program. The purpose of preliminary interviews is to sort candidates, deciding who merits a longer, on-site interview.

How can you get the most out of a job fair? Teacher job fairs are held on college campuses, and in school districts. The job fair is a time to recruit teachers, remembering those high-needs fields like math, special education, and the sciences. Recruiting candidates at a campus job fair is good public relations, increasing the possibility of finding some strong potential candidates.

In addition to the professional human resources staff, sending a principal or teacher to the job fair can prove very useful. Candidates like to talk with their potential employers directly—the decentralized model of hiring—and they like to talk with teachers about the realities of working in the district.

When time permits, use job fairs for short, preliminary interviews. The interview questions should be written in advance, preferably on an evaluation form, and should be used in the exact order with each candidate interviewed. Using the BBI-style of interviewing, questions should ask for past experience about specific teaching situations. Sample preliminary interview questions follow:

1. Tell about your best teaching experience.
2. Describe a lesson that you have taught recently and why it went well.
3. Explain a classroom management system or plan that you have used and how it worked.
4. Describe the daily procedures and routines in a classroom where you have worked.
5. What parts of your teacher education training have you used the most?

6. What do you know about our district, and what is your interest in working here?

If time permits, add questions about the Common Core Standards, and specifics about the elementary, middle, or high school position that is open. While still preliminary in nature, telephone and online interviews are somewhat different than those at job fairs. These interviews are longer and will include more questions specific to the position.

No matter the venue of the interview, all questions should be written in advance, and used in the same order with all candidates. It can be argued that asking different questions of different candidates is discriminatory, as each candidate did not have the same opportunity to present his/her skills for the position. If teachers are used for any of these interviews, providing training and sample questions will help them to better complete their work.

With regard to the validity of evidencing that this style of questioning will gain more effective teachers than a nonformal style of interviewing, more definitive research is still needed. However, using questions that are specific to the skills and expertise needed to be an effective teacher does increase the likelihood of the selection of an effective teacher.

While any candidate can form an answer to a hypothetical situation, a candidate who can articulate an answer where he/she has experienced a situation and been successful in that teaching situation is much more likely to have success when hired. Research from the business world supports the premise that a competency-based interview, such as one with BBI-style questions, can result in a stronger, more competent hire (Kessler, 2006).

On-Site Interview Protocol and Questions

Mindful of the fact that today's teacher candidates want to be feel wooed, the on-site interview remains the best way to assess a candidate's effectiveness and to recruit them. Some reminders include:

1. It must be clear when the candidate is to arrive, who will greet them, and how long their interview day will be.
2. Candidates should know with whom they will be interviewing. Give them a schedule.
3. Staff must be welcoming and business-like with the candidate.
4. School tours are important. Candidates want to see where their classrooms will be located and what technology is in use.
5. If possible, plan a visit to observe in a classroom.
6. There shouldn't be surprises. A candidate should know if they are interviewing with a group of grade-level teachers. They should know if more than one candidate is interviewing at the same time. (Some

districts have two to three candidates interview with a group of interviewers at once to observe collegial interaction.)

7. It is good to provide a hiring timeline, letting candidates know when they may hear back.
8. Do not reveal information about other candidates who have already been interviewed or who will be interviewed, although some candidates ask about their competition!

Specific On-Site Interview Questions

It is during the on-site interview that the use of behavior-based interview style questions is perhaps the most useful. Questions can be crafted to the specific experiences and skills needed for a teacher to be successful in a job. The interviewer should look closely at each job, then write the questions needed. For example, if a principal needs a fourth-grade teacher who will work with approximately twenty-six children and supervise a paraprofessional, questions are written to those specifications. Add questions about the demographics of the district, and about working with special education teachers, if those considerations are applicable. For this specific job, prewritten questions might include:

1. Tell us about your work experience with upper elementary students.
2. Describe a former classroom where you have worked, with regard to student demographics.
3. How have you supervised a paraprofessional in a classroom? Share specific examples of what the parapro did to assist you in teaching.
4. What is your experience with special education students in a regular education classroom, supported by a part-time special education teacher in the room?

After these questions, or before, the general BBI-style questions about all of the other teaching topics are included. For example:

1. Describe a typical lesson plan that you have written. What were the components of the plan and how did you implement it?
2. Tell us about positive classroom management procedures and routines that you have seen or used.
3. Elaborate on classroom management. What kinds of rules, positives, and consequences have you used in a management plan?
4. How have you assessed students formally and informally?
5. What has been your approach to preparing students for standardized tests?
6. How have you successfully communicated with families?

7. Tell about a success story with an underachieving student.
8. How have you differentiated a lesson to reach all students?
9. Can you begin work on _____?
10. What remaining questions do you have for us?

(See appendices 3.2 to 3.7 for banks of questions for all teaching fields.)

It is argued that candidates who can talk about their past experience and expertise on the topics of teaching are much more likely to be able to implement the skills needed in the classroom when hired. This style of interviewing makes the process of selection much "more than a gut feeling" (Deems, 1994, p. 8).

Imagine asking a candidate how they have organized a previous classroom, in terms of procedures and routines. When the candidate responds, "Well, it wasn't always organized, but every day I tried to get students to settle down and work." This candidate clearly has no idea of how to implement procedures and routines, and will not know how to do so if hired.

Multiple Interviews Determine Effectiveness

A job fair interview combined with a well-planned Skype or phone interview should narrow the selection process to those who will be interviewed on-site. On-site interviews should also be conducted by multiple people. Building-level administrators need to interview the candidates thoroughly. Interview questions should be written out in advance, with the exact same set of questions used with each candidate. The use of teachers in the interview process is growing, and teacher input on candidate selection can be very useful. However, teachers need training in how to interview.

Just as some teachers "teach the way that they were taught," some administrators may "hire the way that they were hired." All involved in the hiring of teachers should have both initial and ongoing training. The topics of training include legal issues, how to develop and write questions that determine if a candidate has the skills for the job, how to evaluate answers, how to recruit while interviewing, and how to assist with the process from decision making to finalizing a contract with a candidate.

A first issue in training is that of the legalities and illegalities of hiring. For example, a principal may not promise a job to any candidate without following the hiring process guidelines of the district. While administrators involved in hiring are aware of the federal guidelines that do not permit discussion of a candidate's race, religion, native language, disabilities, or family or marital status, some do not know that *everyone* who meets a candidate must abide by these guidelines.

It is completely prohibited for an office receptionist to ask a candidate certain personal questions and doing so may open the district to great difficulty. Asking about a cast on an ankle is prohibited, as it can be considered a question relating to disability. Commenting on a candidate's attire, jewelry, or hairstyle should never be done, as these may be indicative of race or religion.

What is considered small talk is not small talk in an interview session and may be considered discriminatory questioning. The questions and discussions with candidates at all times should be about their experience and expertise for doing the job of teaching.

When planning for the training of those involved in hiring, consider sharing journal articles or books in discussion sessions. Role-playing is a good way to generate discussion, as well.

Training of teachers in the interview process includes what to ask and what not to ask. If a group of teachers interviews the candidate, someone must guide the time and monitor questions. Reminders must be taught to all who interview about prohibited questions. Consider the following for using groups of teachers to interview:

1. Questions may NOT be asked about any of the following: nationality, race, gender, sexual preference, family, children, religion, or disabilities.
2. If a candidate volunteers information about one of the above prohibited topics, the interviewer may not ask a follow-up question. For example: If a candidate says that her spouse has just relocated to this city, the employer may not ask about the spouse's position or work.
3. List the questions specific to the grade or subject area of the position opening. Note how descriptive comments about the school can be added to questions.

   - In our school, we use the XXX reading program. Tell us about your experience teaching reading.
   - Our classes generally include a percentage of _____ (English language learners, special education students, low socioeconomic students). Describe your experience with this population group.
   - Our principal is great to schedule time for us to plan as departments. Tell us about your experience working with colleagues on planning.
   - This school has an excellent reputation for strong test scores. How have you worked with students to raise their achievement?
   - What interests you most about teaching here? What special talents might you bring to the grade level/department?

As time permits, having candidates teach a mini-lesson to students is worthwhile. If teaching a lesson is part of the interview, determine in advance who will observe the candidates as they teach. Create a useful evaluation tool for both the teachers who observe the lesson and the students who are taught. Evaluative questions for the teacher observers include:

1. Did the candidate teach in developmentally appropriate ways for the age group of students?
2. Did the lesson have an introduction, new material, some student interaction, and a conclusion?
3. Did the candidate project a teacher voice and was he/she easy to understand?
4. Did the candidate seem energetic and enthusiastic?

For students in the class:

1. This teacher interested me in the lesson.	Yes	No
2. This teacher seemed to know the material.	Yes	No
3. I think I would like a class with this teacher.	Yes	No

Comments:

It is important to decide how the input of teachers and students will be used by the administrators who make the final hiring decisions. While it is best to get multiple measures of candidates' expertise, not all who interview or observe will agree. It is best to remind teachers that their input is important, but advisory, if that is the case.

Evaluation of Candidates' Answers

Every question asked should be one that can be evaluated. Additionally, the interviewer should know what to listen for with each answer. Using the mnemonics of PAR and STAR, guide the listener when evaluating answers. PAR stands for "problem, action, and result." If a question asks for input about dealing with a challenging classroom management issue, the best answer would be one where the candidate can describe a problem encountered, the action taken to solve the issue, and the result.

STAR is similar, but the question does not have to be about a problem. STAR represents "situation, task, action, and result." When asked, "Describe your experience using the foreign language exclusively in the classroom," a strong candidate will discuss how they did this, and the result. A STAR answer follows:

During my student teaching (S), I saw how important it was to have "Spanish Only" sections of class, or even days of class (T). My wonderful cooperating teacher taught me ways to do this. She had a big sign that she posted in the front of the room when only Spanish was spoken (A), and it said, "Español ahora." Amazingly, that sign worked! I learned that if I use as much of the language as possible all of the time, and if I teach survival phrases early in the year, my students will speak more Spanish with this approach. They really can learn more this way (R).

While PAR and STAR help the interviewer to listen for appropriate answers, an evaluation instrument is needed to objectively assess the candidate's responses. An easy evaluation system is to create three categories next to each written question. The categories are unacceptable, acceptable, and target. After listening to the candidate's answers, a simple check is made in the appropriate category. When tallying the checks, a candidate with the most target answers has evidenced the most knowledge and experience for that position.

Some employers want numbers for the evaluation instrument, and then a scale of 1 to 5 or 1 to 7 is used. The number 1 indicates a very weak answer, or little to no experience with the topic of the question, while the highest number indicates a very strong answer. Other employers seek a system with three categories, unacceptable, acceptable, or target/outstanding answer. To gain even more specific information, a rubric can be developed for evaluation of candidates' answers. (See appendices 3.8 and 3.9 for sample evaluation tools.)

Consider the following guideline for the evaluation of one typical question:

Question: How have you planned formal and informal assessments to measure student mastery of instructional goals?

Exemplary/Outstanding Answer

The candidate provides concrete past examples of using assessment to develop learning goals, inform instruction, and guide students in their learning. The candidate shares samples from a portfolio, or describes consistent, exemplary use of communicating assessment results with parents, students, and other teachers or administrators. The candidate's answers indicate continual use of assessment to inform delivery of instruction and to help students.

Proficient/Acceptable Answer

The candidate's answers indicate systematic and consistent use of assessment to measure student progress and to inform instructional content and delivery. The candidate can describe a past experience about sharing assessments with parents and students, and indicates knowledge of the vocabulary of uses of assessment.

Developing/Needs Development

The candidate's answers indicate limited knowledge of the vocabulary of assessment uses and limited experience using assessment to inform practice. The candidate is not consistent in the use of feedback to students and has limited experience communicating assessment results to others, including parents.

Unacceptable

The candidate does not recognize the need to use assessment tools to improve teaching practice, to measure student progress, or to provide feedback in a timely manner. He/she has almost no experience with assessment uses.

Based on this one example, the use of the rubric further defines what the employer seeks in answers. However, building a pool of rubric-style criteria can be time-consuming.

Final Decisions

Having a set of evaluation instruments guides those who make final decisions. Hiring should be based on the abilities of the candidate to do the job assigned. Once a decision is made, and an offer accepted, then the district begins the process of induction of the new hire. Induction begins as soon as the candidate is hired, not on the first day of work.

Clear communication with new hires about employment paperwork, insurance, and orientation can result in a more satisfied new employee. Teachers should feel that they were recruited, and no new hire should ever hear that he/she was not a first choice. What happens during the hiring process should not be shared with employees.

While many employers view the interview process as a way to select and sort the best new hires, many candidates consider the interview the time to decide if they want to work for the school district. Interviewers should always be courteous and respectful. An administrator who takes phone calls during an interview is telling the candidate that he/she is too busy to give them much attention. This candidate may presume that the boss will have even less time to support them when hired.

School tours are a good way to recruit teachers by showing them the rooms where they will teach and the technology available. Some candidates may decide that they do not want a job after the school tour, because the building appears dirty and classrooms are in disrepair. The school as a workplace can be a great recruitment tool or a detractor. Culture is a huge factor in recruiting today's Millennial teacher candidates.

Perhaps the best recruitment tool is to advertise a strong teacher induction and mentoring program during the interview process. New hires want to know that they are supported in their future jobs. They also want to know about affordable housing and the services offered in the community. Consider having someone from the human resources office provide this information, along with salary and benefits.

ASSESSMENT OF HIRING PRACTICE

Many district-level administrators are so thrilled that all positions have been filled that they rarely plan to assess the year's hiring practice, but continual evaluation of hiring is a necessary step. By surveying the new hires, employers gain insightful information. (See appendix 3.10 for a survey template to use.)

Will new hires be honest about their hiring, since they may be concerned that saying anything negative will effect rehiring decisions? Some may be overly positive, but Millennials seem to be very concerned about the organizations where they work. This generation of teachers wants their voices heard, and surveying them about their hiring experiences may be seen as a vehicle for them to respectfully make their suggestions for improvement.

Surveying those involved in the process of hiring is also useful. (See appendix 3.11 for a sample.) Consider seeking feedback about hiring and induction from strong teachers who have attained tenure. These effective teachers can provide valuable information about their success and can become an integral part of assisting new hires. When feedback is sought on an annual basis, patterns for improvement should emerge. A key is to study the plan—this blueprint created—and to strive for continual updating.

SUMMARY POINTS FOR SUCCESS

1. Hiring is a year-round job. Define the roles for all involved in your plan and train all involved in the interview process.
2. Advertise widely, remembering that today's teacher candidates want quick responses to their applications.
3. Use behavior-based interviewing as a way to ascertain the candidate's experience and expertise. Avoid hypothetical, funny, or "gotcha" questions.
4. Write out all interview questions in advance, with an evaluation system for judging the quality of the answers.

5. Use the quantitative data gathered from the prewritten interview questions with assessments to make final decisions.
6. Retention of the most effective teachers begins with hiring.

Chapter Four

Best Practices in Orientation

Novice teachers are often left to sink or swim—but it doesn't have to be that way.

—Jeremiah Hill (2004, paragraph 1)

Generally described as "onboarding" in the business world, induction is critically important to new teacher success and retention. "Induction" is an umbrella term used to describe all aspects of bringing a new hire into the organization. Induction for new teachers generally includes orientation, mentoring, and ongoing professional development. While virtually all districts do some form of orientation, this chapter discusses both the orientation that teachers receive before back-to-school workshops, and what is generally considered orientation.

A district retention plan needs to outline the aspects of orientation, and to budget for the time and personnel to conduct the orientations. Adding an assessment component to orientation provides continual feedback for improvement. Using district teachers to share their best practice experiences not only saves money, but also rewards teachers and provides them with leadership experiences that lead to their own retention. Supportive orientation shows that the district values new and experienced employees. Building the positive school culture begins with orientation practices.

STEPS OF ORIENTATION

When an administrator hires a new teacher, orientation actually begins. In the initial contact to offer the job, the employer can explain the next steps. First-time teachers may not understand what a letter of intent is or that they are not officially hired until the school board meets. Explanations of the process ease new hire frustrations.

Consider everything that happens between hiring and the first day of student attendance to be orientation. Keeping in contact with new hires is critical. E-mail is a good way to communicate, but consider a password-protected social media site just for the new cohort of teachers. On this site, which is a subset of the district's website, teachers can get updates on the back-to-school orientation dates, room assignments, and reminders of the paperwork they must complete before school begins. Is there a way that new hires can check on the status of their completed insurance forms, payroll forms, and background checks? Doing all of this electronically before the start of school saves much stress.

In this pre-orientation stage, teachers will appreciate help with life is-sues—particularly housing. When a district provides a list of realtors and available apartments, it is appreciated. In 2015 the San Francisco Unified School District began an ambitious plan to build a housing complex just for teachers. Additionally, low-interest loans were available for teachers, and a housing bonus paid after ten years of employment (Green and Knight, 2015). Imagine the support that teachers feel from this type of help. It is indeed a retention builder for teachers.

More pre-orientation is needed when hiring teachers new to the city or area. Special pre-orientation may be needed for those joining the faculty from out-of-state or a foreign country. For those hires who are completely new to the state, consider a special summer orientation that stresses the following topics about living:

1. The demographics of the community and area
2. Available housing (bring in community help—realtors, chamber of commerce, etc.)
3. When and how to get utilities, phones, internet provider, and so forth
4. Special events and community activities of interest
5. A tour of the area, including a tour of a plant or significant employer in the area
6. Information about insurance, clinics, hospitals, shopping, and banking
7. Out-of-country hires may need special assistance with visas, housing agreements, and cultural issues specific to the area

Strive to make the event truly welcoming, with a breakfast or lunch provided by a local service club. Give out gift bags and door prizes donated by local businesses.

Orientation Before the Start of School

Here is what NOT to do in a back-to-school orientation program for new hires.

1. Do not make teachers sit in a hot auditorium or cafeteria and listen to speakers say a welcome message six different ways.
2. Do not have speakers read the handbook to new teachers.
3. Do not make teachers stay in meetings when they need to work in their classrooms to get things organized.
4. Do not make all teachers sit through the orientation together. High school teaching is quite different than teaching second grade!
5. Do not hire an expensive presenter to provide a motivational talk when district teachers can provide more pertinent training.
6. Do not try to provide all the professional development training to new teachers in one, two, or even three days of workshops before the year starts. Provide the most relevant information and plan on continued seminars for training throughout the first year.

Where should administrators start in their planning of orientation that supports the retention of new teachers? The following are planning considerations:

1. Who will plan the orientation programs?
2. Who will teach the programming?
3. Are funds available to pay those who teach in the orientation program and for the new hires who attend additional days before the start of the paid contractual days? (Remember that "cash and culture" matter to new hires. Paying a simple honorarium is very beneficial to new teachers, both for financial reasons and for morale.)
4. Where will orientation be held and how will new hires be divided for their sessions?
5. How will active learning and engagement strategies be implemented in the orientation sessions?
6. How long will new teacher orientation be?
7. How much of the orientation time will be allotted for teachers to work in their classrooms with their mentors?
8. How will orientation be evaluated? (See appendix 4.1 for a sample evaluation.)

Building the Agenda for Orientation

Time is a precious commodity for administrators and for teachers. Build the orientation schedule to provide just enough information to allow teachers to feel ready, yet not overwhelmed, for the first day of school. What they need is "just in time" learning. Consider the following must-have information:

1. The school calendar and where to find the updates online.
2. How to use the school/district website and new teacher discussion board for questions.
3. Deadlines for the first grading cycle and a brief overview of the school's technology supports. (Remember that elementary and middle and secondary teachers should be in separate orientation sessions if at all possible.)
4. Legal issues and updates.
5. Overview of curricular issues, with specifics to be shared by mentors or grade- and subject-level teacher leaders.
6. How the district mentoring program works—what new teachers can and can't expect from a mentor.
7. Special emergency procedures.
8. Classroom management and discipline guidelines.

How do presenters make new teacher orientation engaging? Presenters should always use active learning and engaging strategies. Even introductions can be a teachable moment. Ask participants to introduce themselves as they will to their students on the first day of school. Ask them to say what they will say during the first forty-five seconds of facing their first class. It is a memorable and useful activity for introductions. After all introductions, discuss how important the first moment of the first day of school is, and that teachers should really script out what they should say to students. Harry and Rosemary Wong's book, *The First Days of School* (2012), has ample examples of how to do this.

Instead of pointing out guidelines in the faculty handbook, appeal to the new teachers' sense of teamwork and camaraderie by asking questions and allowing groups to find the answer in the handbook (online or on paper). Give points and award a prize for answers. Example: If you wake up sick one morning, what are our guidelines for contacting your administrator? Teachers work together to find the answer.

Use "make it and take it" ideas. It is often pointless to announce, "You will need a classroom management poster in your room by the end of the first week of school." Instead, have a session where a group of veteran teachers show their management plans and provide markers and a poster to each teacher to make their own during the session.

Emergency situations must be discussed, as should violence prevention procedures. Plan time for role-playing "what if" scenarios. (See appendix 4.2.) Role-playing is also good for working with a mentor and for how to talk with parents.

New teacher orientation should be at least three days long, or perhaps a week. However, these large group sessions will probably be evaluated lower than work time given to teachers to work in their classrooms. Building in time for new teachers to organize and work in their classrooms, with the help of their trained mentor, is generally rated very highly by new teachers.

While the next chapter of this book explains building new teacher and mentor relationships, time must be allotted during orientation for simply explaining the mentoring program to the new hires. Providing written guidelines to the teachers about what a mentor can and can't do is helpful. A panel made up of previous new teachers and their mentors will also be an excellent springboard for discussion. Invite second- and third-year teachers and their mentors to serve on the panel. Consider the following questions to start the discussion, and then allow for questions from the new hires:

1. What was the most helpful thing that you and your mentor did together?
2. How did you find time to work together?
3. Did working with a mentor ever feel uncomfortable? Why? How did you overcome that challenge?
4. For the mentors: What is the single best piece of advice you give new teachers?
5. For the mentors: What are you not supposed to do and what shouldn't we ask of you?
6. Is there really confidentiality between the mentor and new teacher? If I report something really odd that I have done, how do I know it won't be reported to my boss?

The more orientation that can be provided up front about the mentoring program, the more effective mentoring can be.

INDIVIDUALIZING ORIENTATION

Mentoring is one way to individualize the orientation of new hires, as mentors should generally be in the same grade and/or subject level as their mentee/new teacher. Other ways to differentiate orientation are to provide only a portion of orientation for the whole group of new hires, and then divide the group for grade levels. Large districts may have the opportunity to further divide teachers into groups of new hires and hires with a certain number of years of experience.

Providing get-acquainted activities and same-group meetings provides a starting point for having the teachers develop their own support groups. Millennial hires seek teams, and positive bonding experiences in orientation will help them to survive and thrive as teachers. Help new teachers form groups across building lines, such as having all the district's new math teachers meet together during orientation. They can exchange e-mail addresses, or set up their own social media site just for new math teachers. One administrator considers each new cohort of hires like a pledge class in a campus sorority or fraternity and gets very positive results.

If at all possible, new teacher orientation should include defined work time in the teacher's classroom to further individualize orientation. Outcomes for the work time should be given. For example:

At the end of new teacher orientation, the following should be completed in the classroom:

1. Chairs should be arranged with clear walking spaces and accessibility. While all chairs do not have to be in rows, chairs should face the front so that students can see the visuals and the teacher. Students should not have to turn to see instruction.
2. A classroom management plan with rules, consequences, and positive reinforcements should be posted in the classroom.
3. Emergency procedures should be posted.
4. The teacher should have his/her name posted and have a welcoming sign or visual ready.
5. The teacher needs to have procedures posted for entering and leaving the room.
6. The teacher needs a scripted introduction/lesson plan/PowerPoint for teaching the procedures for the first day.
7. A first-day activity should be ready—such as an interest inventory or pretest.
8. A first-day lesson should be ready. It should be engaging and interesting.
9. A plan for class dismissal and/or getting students to lunch or buses must be ready.
10. Getting acquainted activities for learning names work well during the first week. Have some ready.
11. Know where the student restrooms are and what the procedure is for using a restroom.
12. Know who to contact for an emergency question.

Mentors can go over this list with new teachers or administrators can do a quick walk-through evaluation to see that a classroom is ready. One administrator gave awards (gift cards for Starbucks coffee) for those with the most prepared classrooms the day before students arrived. While being prepared should not necessarily be a competition, new hires, and those returning, need to be aware of the value of having the classroom ready. There really is no such thing as being over-prepared when one is a teacher, and teachers only get one chance to make a first impression.

SUMMARY POINTS FOR SUCCESS

1. Employees at McDonalds are paid for their training and orientation. Strive to find the funding to pay new hires and their mentors for extra days of work before the regular back-to-school programs. Even gift cards for school supplies are appreciated.
2. Make orientation useful by modeling teaching strategies in sessions and allowing time for working in classrooms.
3. Hold teachers and their mentors accountable for orientation time and activities. Give checklists and follow up with visits to classrooms before students arrive.
4. Individualize orientation as much as possible. New teachers with no experience need a different orientation than new hires with much experience from another district.
5. Provide some positive reinforcement during orientation—provide snacks, lunches, and prizes. Engage new hires with each other. Help them form their own support team.

Chapter Five

Mentoring Programs

A mentor is a guide and trusted friend, but not someone to do your photocopying.

—Anonymous teacher in mentor training session

"Mentoring" can be defined in the teaching profession as "the personal guidance provided, usually by seasoned veteran teachers, to beginning teachers in schools" (Smith and Ingersoll, 2004, p. 683). Mentoring has been classically defined as "a deliberate pairing of a more skilled or experienced person with a lesser skilled or experienced one, with the agreed-upon goal of having the lesser skilled person grow and develop specific competencies" (Murray, 1991, xiv).

While some use the terms "induction" and "mentoring" interchangeably, mentoring is just a part of the induction process, as induction includes orientation and ongoing professional development for new hires. Mentoring is certainly not specific to the teaching profession, and anyone who has received supportive mentoring will attest to its benefits.

Research on mentoring programs for new teachers has generally indicated that the new teachers' attitudes and retention can be influenced by positive mentoring. Attitudes can include job satisfaction, efficacy, and commitment (Smith and Ingersoll, 2004). A teacher who feels supported in his/her work can be more effective, leading to higher student achievement. A bonus effect is that "quality mentoring improves the mentor's performance, too" (Sweeny, 2008, p.5).

If, as Sweeny suggests, 96 percent of new teachers can be retained with quality mentoring, and if "not providing mentoring has a negative impact on the quality of teaching" (2008, p. 5), then why isn't mentoring an integral component of all school districts? Mentoring has to be prioritized, and it has to be planned. Mentoring must be a year-round commitment with regard to

41

the training of mentors, assigning them to new hires, planning time and resources for mentor/new teacher work, and evaluation of the program.

IMPLEMENTING A MENTORING PROGRAM

As with any program, the mentoring piece of induction must be planned, and the plans need to be written. Big questions to start the discussion include:

1. Who will be chosen to mentor and how will they be selected?
2. In our district, do we need to negotiate the mentoring piece into the teachers' contract, according to union/professional organization guidelines?
3. Who will be responsible for leading the program at district and building levels?
4. When and how will time be allotted for initial and follow-up training of mentors?
5. What will the budget look like for the program?
6. What will the role of the mentors be? Will they be supportive only, or will they have a supervisory/evaluative role?
7. How can time be allocated for mentors and new teachers to work together?

Hundreds of mentor programs exist in the United States. Each district does not have to reinvent the wheel and create all of its own materials from scratch. Use the books and guidelines already published. (See, for example, Sweeny, 2008, and Clement and Wilkins, 2011.)

To begin, or update, a mentoring program, consider a small advisory committee to brainstorm ideas and develop the blueprint for the program. Teachers must be included on the committee, as programs with teacher buy-in will be better accepted by all teachers than one that comes as a mandate from administration.

Consider the following timeline for what to do during a year.

January–March: Create or update the mentor program guidelines.

- Select new mentors for the next school year.
- Plan the new mentor training; select the resource book(s) for the mentors.
- When mentors are already in place, they need time to continue work with new teachers.
- Check that current mentors observe and provide specific instructional feedback to new teachers.

April–June: Schedule new mentor training (at least three days)

- Evaluate the training.
- Provide evaluation and refresher training of past mentors.
- Plan a celebration for last year's mentors and new teachers.
- Program director begins pairing mentors with new hires.

July–August: Pairings of mentors and new teachers are completed

- Mentors and new teachers meet and get acquainted in orientation.
- Mentors work with new teachers several half-days before students arrive, usually setting up classrooms.

September–December: Critically important time for mentors to guide new hires

- Mentors should observe in the new teacher's classroom.
- New teachers should observe mentors.
- Allow time for mentor and new teacher pairings to attend a workshop together.
- Allow time for pairs to simply reflect and discuss teaching.

What Mentors Need to Know

The skill set needed to teach third graders is a different skill set than the one needed to teach another adult how to teach third grade. What makes a good mentor? A mentor needs to be consciously competent. This means that they must know how to teach and how to explain their instructional skills to someone else. Mentor selection and training facilitate the creation of consciously competent mentors.

To select the best mentors, ask for applications. (See appendix 5.1.) Select teachers who exhibit a positive attitude about the profession, who are able to encourage their colleagues, and who achieve academic success with their own students. The mentors must receive training in their role and administrative expectations, their accountability, and the specifics of topics they need to address with new hires.

By choosing a good textbook on mentor training and combining that with materials that already exist in the district, such as the faculty handbook, the mentor training does not have to be developed from scratch. (In addition to materials already suggested, see, for example, Portner, 2008; Boreen, Johnson, Niday, and Potts, 2009; and Richin, Banyon, Stein, and Banyon, 2003).

Like any effective professional development, mentor training takes time, and should take place over a period of time. Consider three days of training spread out over a three-week time frame. Intense days of training may work at the end of a school year, to renew and refresh the mentors themselves. Mentor training should include:

1. Roles and responsibilities of mentors: what you can and can't do
2. Legal issues for the mentors; accountability
3. How adults learn best
4. The timeline for meeting with new teachers; what will happen when
5. How to teach the "hot topics" of the school and district
6. How to teach stress management and time management to the new hires
7. How to teach classroom management
8. The value of observations; clinical observation practices
9. When to be direct with a new hire and when to be collaborative or indirect
10. How to find time to be an effective mentor; mentor time and stress management
11. Discussions with former mentors and/or recent new teachers
12. Role-playing about possible situations

Involving teachers in the mentor training can be very useful. A panel of past mentors can answer questions and provide practical advice. A panel of recent new hires can talk about what they learned from the mentors and what they needed for support. If mentoring is new to the district, consider a panel of veteran teachers to provide insights, as well as a panel of new teachers. Take advantage of highly effective teachers to share the hot topic issues during mentor training.

Mentor training may be seen by some educators as a reward for their hard work and expertise. The stipend or honoraria paid may be seen as a bonus. For a few teachers, working as a mentor may also be seen as a way to move up the ladder to a professional development or administrative position. Feeling valued and appreciated is important to all teachers.

Whenever possible, provide snacks, meals, and free teaching supplies. A certificate and a letter in their personnel file is another important way to express appreciation. Being a mentor is another way to retain highly effective teachers, as mentoring is a means for teachers to grow professionally and still stay in the classroom.

Mentor training should not be limited to the initial training. Follow-up training can be as simple as an occasional discussion group with coffee and snacks. Mentors need to de-brief about their own stress and the issues of supporting new hires. If a significant change happens in the district, such as new standards, new testing, or a violent event, mentors can be informed quickly and can then share that information with newer employees. Mentor training, whether initial or follow-up, needs continual evaluation. (See appendix 5.2.)

USING MENTOR TEAMS AND LONG-TERM MENTORING

Paraphrasing the old adage, "It takes a village to raise a child," does it take more than one mentor to support a new teacher? How would mentors share their duties, and would a mentor team be of most use for mentoring over a long time frame, such as the first five years of a teacher's career?

In Singapore, known for its high student achievement rates, new hires are given time to "plan, observe other teachers, talk with their assigned senior teacher mentor, and meet with their teacher buddy." Additionally, "New teachers are observed and coached by grade-level chairs, subject-area chairs, and department heads" (Sclafani, 2015, p. 10). This is indeed a village approach.

Assigning a junior mentor to a new hire can be very useful. This mentor may be in their first five years of teaching and will be well aware of the new teacher's issues. Millennial employees may appreciate the viewpoint of this less formal mentor who is nearer to them in age. Even though the role is less formal, a young mentor still needs mentor training with regard to their roles and responsibility. Is it their role to take the new hire out for a drink after a bad formal evaluation? Where is the line between less formal mentoring and professional support? Some training with discussion time is needed to guide this type of mentoring as well.

Consider the following questions for a panel discussion with junior mentors:

1. As a young, or new-to-the-profession teacher yourself, what do you have to offer a new hire?
2. What were some of your biggest surprises during your first or second year of teaching?
3. How did you achieve good time management to survive and thrive when first hired?
4. How did you handle a bad day when first hired? How do you handle a bad day now?
5. What was a huge challenge when you started teaching?
6. Describe a specific success with a specific student and how you made that success happen.
7. How did your mentor help you in your first year and beyond?
8. What professional development (PD) helped you the most? Where did you receive that PD?

9. Tell about your long-term teaching plans in this district. What factors have helped you make the decision to stay here?
10. What is one piece of advice you would always give a new hire?

Second and third years of classroom teaching may be prime times for actually making an impact on the new teacher's instruction. The first year is just survival, and a strong new hire feels more open about trying new strategies and implementing more technology once he/she has survived. Once the new teacher's confidence level has increased, then a bit of experimentation and risk-taking may be more appropriate.

What might a complete five-year mentoring program look like for the new hire?

Year One:

- The formal mentor meets with the new teacher and helps to organize the classroom. Three half-days of work in the new teacher's room take place before students arrive.
- The mentor and new teacher have a twenty-minute conversation every week. They follow guidelines for what to discuss. (See appendix 5.3.)
- The mentor observes the new teacher at least three times during the first year.
- The new teacher observes the mentor at least three times during the year.
- Together, the new teacher and mentor choose one area of teaching to concentrate their conversations and observations on, such as classroom management or reading.
- The new teacher has a junior mentor. They talk as needed, but at least once every two weeks.
- The new teacher and the junior mentor may choose to observe in each other's classrooms as time permits.
- The new teacher and both mentors keep a log of time spent together and topics discussed, without evaluative comments.

Year Two:

- Before school starts, the mentor and new teacher discuss at least two issues as their key goals for improvement.
- The mentor and new teacher talk bi-weekly for at least twenty minutes.
- The mentor observes the new teacher at least twice.
- The new teacher observes another teacher at least twice to observe about the goals listed for the year.

- The mentor and the new teacher, or the junior mentor and the new teacher attend a professional workshop or meeting together.
- The new teacher and the junior mentor talk at least bi-weekly.

Year Three:

- Together with both mentors, and/or a department chair, the new teacher writes at least three professional goals and action steps for their completion.
- At this stage of mentoring, the times and guidelines for mentoring may be much less formal, but the relationship should still exist so that the third-year teacher does not feel isolated.

Years Four and Five:

- During years four and five, the mentors should encourage their teacher to take on a leadership role, such as serving as a junior mentor, or leading a curriculum unit in the grade/subject level.
- Conversations do not have to have set meeting times, but conversations should definitely continue.
- New teachers should be encouraged to complete an advanced degree or to consider an administrative degree for continued work in schools.
- New teachers and their mentors should attend professional conferences and meetings together. They should consider writing about their work and presenting workshops.
- It may be important to have conversations about teaching as a long-time career. Can mentors introduce their teacher to others who can help them to achieve their goals?

Obstacles to Be Overcome in Mentoring

The first obstacle to be overcome in mentoring is the trust issue with new hires. Some new hires may feel that their mentor is the principal's eyes and ears, and may have difficulty confiding in, or even talking with, their mentors. Some new hires may not believe that they even need a mentor and may resent having another teacher observing in their room. It is not uncommon for a new teacher to simply want to be left alone to teach.

To overcome these potential obstacles, discuss mentoring in the interview and orientation processes. How a candidate reacts to the information about the mentoring program may be a red flag indicating how he/she will react to other collaborative or evaluative processes.

There are costs involved in developing and maintaining an effective mentoring program. Programs must have directors, and adding the leadership component for mentoring to an administrator's job may mean that person's other duties are distributed. With distribution of duties comes more cost.

If mentor training takes place during the school year, substitute teachers must be paid to cover classes. If training occurs outside of the school day or school year, teachers must be remunerated. The cost for materials, books, food, and secretarial support for the training must be budgeted. If an outside trainer is hired, costs rise very quickly.

In some districts, the administration must pay new hires for the days of orientation before school starts, or before the regular back-to-school programs begin. If mentors are used to work with the new hires during those days, they must be paid. Attending training and workshops together can be very beneficial for both new teachers and their mentors, but travel and expenses for professional development continue to rise.

The obstacles are many and costly, but the desired result is a more collegial workplace, where teacher isolation is limited. Ongoing mentoring is one way to change school culture, and as discussed earlier in this book, both cash and culture count when striving to retain effective teachers. Administrators will need to know the research on the value of mentoring—and especially of extended mentoring—in order to seek funding and support for these programs.

MENTOR PROGRAM EVALUATION

As outlined in this chapter, mentor programs need time and money to succeed. Upper-level district administrators and school boards will expect accountability and results from the programs. Documentation of the work done by mentors and of the time spent working with new teachers are ways to show that the time and money have been used. How might the program be evaluated with regard to overall effectiveness?

Simple surveys of both the new teachers and the mentors regarding the program provide some quantitative and qualitative data. (See appendices 5.4 and 5.5.) Action research may be implemented to look at specific questions. Consider having a veteran teacher in a graduate program conduct his/her research on the mentoring program. What questions can be addressed?

1. Has implementation of mentoring helped retain teachers in the first two, three, or X years? (Look at past data on retention and compare to a new cohort.)
2. Have test scores of students in the classrooms of teachers in their first years of teaching improved when mentoring was implemented?

3. Do teachers report more satisfaction in their jobs after the implementation of mentoring? (Survey research, or use of data such as fewer sick days may be considered.)
4. Do principals feel mentoring has improved the collegiality of teachers? (Surveys or interviews for collection of data are needed.)

As the mentoring program is evaluated, it is important to always get the input of the new hires, their mentors, and of the principals. Data-driven decision making has been a buzzword for years in education, and having documentation and data to support a mentoring program will be critically useful in securing funding and personnel for future programs.

SUMMARY POINTS FOR SUCCESS

1. It has been said that it is better to not have a mentoring program than to use untrained mentors. Offer initial training and ongoing support for the mentors in the district's program.
2. The skills needed to mentor new teachers are different from the skills needed to teach children. Effective mentors know this and work with new teachers in a collegial manner.
3. Strong mentors invite new teachers to observe model lessons in their classrooms and provide supportive, collegial observations in the new teachers' classes.
4. Evaluation of a mentor program is crucial to ensure future funding and support from the district administration.
5. Serving as a mentor can be a leadership role for the veteran teacher, making them feel valued at that stage of their career.

Chapter Six

Professional Development for the First Five Years

> As teachers enter the induction period, they become part of the school learning community that is there to support them and help them learn to be successful teachers.
>
> —Sclafani (2015, summarizing the induction of new teachers in Singapore)

Discussing her first year as a principal, Barker (2015) wrote, "New teachers expect a comprehensive induction system that includes extensive training, resources, and supplies. My mistake was believing that the new teacher orientation my district provided was enough. It wasn't" (p. 7).

New teacher orientation is just a starting point. The real professional development of new hires takes place throughout the first five years. How does the district plan for long-term induction and what role should building-level administration have? Most importantly, how can teachers' individual needs be met and what voice should beginning teachers have in their own professional development?

Data-informed planning is a first step for long-term professional development. Consider a survey each year of the new hires, asking about their strengths. New hires will probably not want to report weaknesses and asking about areas of improvement is negative. Rather than look at new hire from a deficit view, look at strengths and ask about areas of interest.

Consider the creation of a survey with a list of hot topics and ask new hires to rate their strengths. Next on the survey, ask about areas that are of interest to them. (See appendix 6.1.) Use the survey results to plan the first year of the new teacher induction workshops.

PLANNING CONSIDERATIONS FOR FIRST-YEAR WORKSHOPS

As with any professional development activity, much consideration goes into the planning of the offerings. Who will teach these workshops for new hires? The district's professional development staff is the obvious first choice, but new hires want to hear from veteran teachers and other recent hires, as well. Consider bringing in outside experts as needed, but speaking fees and travel costs add to the expenses of using outside experts. New teacher induction workshops must have a leader who knows the knowledge base of beginning teacher concerns and who also knows how to teach and motivate people.

When do teachers find the time to attend? If new teacher workshops are held after school, many teachers will not attend. Can after-school workshops have a special reward to get teachers to attend? Can teachers earn a small stipend for attending? Can they be released from something else as an incentive to attend? When hiring candidates, include information about the ongoing induction supports, and explain the attendance practices.

Should all new hires be required to participate in the induction workshops, or just those who are actually new teachers with one to three years of experience? If the district hires teachers with much experience and strong recommendations, wouldn't they be bored in new teacher training? It is best to make those decisions on a case-by-case basis. An experienced teacher from a different state may need to attend only the workshop on state testing. Having teachers with more than three years of experience choose one or two workshops to attend may be best.

The induction of noncertified, provisionally, or alternatively certified teachers will be planned very differently. These emergency hires may need weekly meetings, as well as specialized mentoring. Teachers who are willing to mentor a fully certified candidate may not want to mentor a noncertified hire, as the time requirements may be overwhelming. Much more direct teaching will be needed from the mentor, the school administrator, and the staff developers if non–fully certified teachers are hired.

Building time into the schedule for induction offerings may work best. One district gave all new hires a half-day of release time once a month (six meetings) for their new teacher workshops the first year. The cost included hiring substitute teachers. The district provided coffee and breakfast, as well as a book, and paid the tuition for each new teacher to earn some college credit for attending. The college credit was an agreement with the neighboring university and an instructor from the university led the seminars, using district personnel as speakers in many sessions.

Historically, teachers have lamented professional development as a waste of time. The seminars must have a curriculum that meets teachers' needs, and the climate of the seminars must be collegial. In fact, the new hires need to bond as a pledge class in a college fraternity/sorority might, in order to support each other throughout their careers in a district. In large districts, the seminars can be at the building level. Another option is to hold discipline-specific induction offerings, such as scheduling time for all new math and science teachers to meet.

Keys for the success of induction workshops include building camaraderie among the participants, providing enough time for open discussions of issues, and enforcing the confidentiality of what is said in those discussions. Another critical issue is not overwhelming the new teachers with "one more thing" that they must do. Meeting once a week is entirely too often. Meeting once or twice a month is about right, especially if the new hires are supported on a day-to-day basis by their mentors.

The Workshop Curriculum

A curriculum for the new teacher induction workshops can be designed around the school year. There are natural topics that emerge during the seasons of the year, as well as the ones gleaned from the new hires' surveys. While new teacher orientation covers many topics, the ongoing offerings should be time specific. Examples follow:

September: Before the first round of parent conferences, plan a workshop on parent communication. (Lesson plan provided in appendix 6.2.) Topics should include:

- How to communicate with families: e-mail, letters, calls
- Social media use: to friend or not to friend the parents
- How to conduct a person-to-person parent conference
- Use role-playing to get new teachers to practice diplomacy in difficult parental situations
- The September session is also a good time to reintroduce the district's evaluation system. Explain when and how classroom observations are completed. Every session should include a short discussion of how the mentoring program is going.

October: Session on classroom management, student behavior, discipline. (Lesson plan provided in appendix 6.3.) While management is addressed in the orientation, new teachers start the year with the "honeymoon" phase where students are pretty well-behaved. Then, after the first grades are delivered, or after homecoming or Halloween, new teachers find managing student behavior to be increasingly difficult. Topics can include:

- What issues do the teachers see during late fall? Have teachers write out a specific management/behavior issue. Then, have other teachers provide possible solutions to those issues.
- Provide specific resources to teachers, such as Canter and Canter's *Succeeding with Difficult Students* (1993) book.
- Show video clips of challenging students and discuss solutions.
- Role-play what to say in challenging situations with students.
- Bring in the resource officer or a special education teacher to share specific behavior management issues.
- Discuss violence prevention in regard to student misconduct.

November: This session can have two parts. The first is preparing for how to handle the holidays, and the second is to choose a specific teaching strategy to emphasize. Consider:

- Discussions about early dismissals and behavior expectations for the days before holiday breaks
- Special guidelines about holiday decorations. Can Christmas decorations be used or not? Are there any specific rules about any holiday topics?
- Choose a specific teaching strategy to introduce at this time. The use of questions and discussions is a good topic. Teachers at all levels need reminders about asking good questions, wait time, and structuring discussions. (See, for example, Walsh and Sattes, 2015.)
- Allow time to celebrate surviving the first semester!

January/February: Throughout the spring semester, teachers have more interest in teaching strategies and test preparation. They have survived and may be more willing to delve into seminar topics more deeply. Early in the spring semester is a good time to present standardized testing issues and test preparation.

- What is the testing schedule and what are the district guidelines?
- What review strategies are common for this district?
- How do I teach test-taking strategies without just teaching to the test?
- Provide information from special education teachers about testing of students with learning/developmental issues.
- Provide information from ESOL teachers about support for English language learners and test preparation.

March: Calendar-appropriate topics for March may include time and stress management, as well as working with underachieving students.

- Begin a workshop with a time management activity. One activity is to have participants draw a circle and fill it in as a pie chart of how they spend a typical school day. They must account for all twenty-four hours in a day. Discuss the charts.
- Have teachers complete a two-column list of their school workday. One column is a list of where they spend too much time and the other is where they want to spend more time. Discuss the lists; then repeat the activity for personal time. Where do people feel that they spend too much time and where would they like to spend more time? What has to happen to make the lists more to their liking?
- The workshop leader can discuss stress management. A starting point is the story of the woman who has tremendous stress every year over cooking Thanksgiving dinner for all of her extended family members. When asked why she has to do this dinner every year, her reply is that she feels she "should." The story ends with the questions, "Why do you 'should' on yourself? How could you lessen the stress? Why can't the family have a potluck at someone else's house or in the church basement?"
- Have participants list and rate their stressors and then make an action plan to change something.

April/May: Teachers need support at this time of the year with the logistics of ending the school year. Topics include:

- How to continue teaching after standardized testing has ended.
- How do we engage students in in-depth project work at the end of the year?
- What are the field trip or senior-year guidelines?
- Allow much time to talk and celebrate the school year.
- Evaluate the seminars and the mentoring program at this time.

Throughout the workshops, open-ended discussion questions guide positive discussions and can dissuade teachers from making the workshops into complaint sessions. Prompts include:

- What is the best thing to happen in your classroom since we last met?
- Describe a student success that made you feel wonderful.
- What issue or problem have you solved recently?

Socializing helps to build cohesiveness. Consider some meetings with coffee and snacks and time to simply talk with the second- or third-year teachers. Some induction seminar time may be used to work with mentors, as well.

If some new teachers are leaving at the end of the first year, or have been released, it may be difficult for them to be positive in a session. Consider a short session with those who are leaving with regard to their participation in the final seminars. It may be best not to have them participate, due to their negativity. Others who are leaving by choice may want the camaraderie. The induction leader needs to recognize the individual differences among teachers and act accordingly.

Evaluation of the seminars is also critically important. If input was sought at the beginning of the program, and that input was not used, teachers will rate the workshops lower. (See appendix 6.4.)

INDUCTION PROGRAMMING FOR YEARS TWO THROUGH FIVE

Beginning teachers often comment that they simply survive the first year, and during the second year and beyond they can absorb and learn more about teaching. What should the induction program look like during the second year?

Professional Learning Communities

During years two through five, offerings for beginning teachers should be ones that lead them from isolation to colleagueship, because feelings of isolation are a factor in teacher dropout. Types of teacher professional development groups vary, including professional learning communities (PLCs), critical friends groups, study groups, research collaboratives, and book study groups.

Professional learning communities take many different shapes, but are based on the premise that teachers can, and need, to learn from each other in collegial groups. A professional learning community has shared leadership, a common vision, and becomes a means for learning as a group (Bond, 2015). To be successful, these groups need resources, the trust of and rapport with members, and the opportunity for sharing teaching practices.

In practical terms, a learning community may want to take a semester, or a whole year, to dig deeper into a hot topic issue of the district. Differentiation could be the focus topic for second-year teachers to study. Because teachers' professional development needs vary widely, several different groups could be formed, and teachers could choose their learning group.

How does the administration guide teacher learning groups? Administrators provide the guidelines, the resources, and the time. They support the groups, yet also assess the outcomes for accountability. Consider the following steps to establish professional learning groups:

1. The administration identifies the director/leader for the communities.

2. The director identifies and invites teachers to serve on a steering committee.
3. The committee surveys teachers to determine needed topics of study. Decisions about who will participate are made.

- Will all second- through fifth-year teachers be in a community of choice?
- Will all teachers with five or fewer years choose to be in a community at least twice in years two through five?

   With topics and participation determined, the groups themselves should form and make their own decisions about the type of study they will complete.

- Is a book the focus of the study? A series of articles?
- Will the teachers complete observations of each other and then discuss as a group?
- Will they review test scores and study areas for improvement?

4. What is the outcome for each group? If the group meetings replace other in-service programs, how will accountability be determined?
5. How will time be provided for the meetings?
   Possible topics:

- Differentiation; special education
- Updating the use of curriculum standards
- ESOL or special population needs
- Specific needs of the teachers regarding a new school or a new program
- Working with parents
- Standardized test scores

6. Administrators work with the groups to implement changes and ideas that are developed and to evaluate the work of the groups for the next year.

Some tremendous work has been developed through structured learning communities. The National Writing Project is one example (Lieberman and Wood, 2002). This project has become a network to foster the development of teachers' learning communities on the topic of the improvement of the teaching of writing. The value of choosing one topic for in-depth study by the teachers who need that area of study is important. Having teachers give input to the topics of their learning, the means by which they learn, and some leadership in the process develops collegiality and an improved school culture. As stated earlier in this book, cash and culture matter in the retention of teachers.

While induction implies that the new teacher is becoming acculturated into the school's world, the first five years of a teacher's career are also a time to develop as beginning teacher leaders. This can happen through leadership of a study group or professional learning community, through organizing a social event, or by becoming a junior mentor to a new hire. Leading a student organization is another way to be a leader. When offering these opportunities to teachers starting their careers, it is important to remember time considerations.

Time Considerations for Induction Programs

How much professional development is too much? Many beginning teachers are struggling to find the time to write lesson plans, grade papers, and simply survive their first few years. They may be newlyweds, young parents, and graduate students. Adding additional meetings and learning communities may be the tipping point for them to say, "I simply can't do all of this." Where does the time come from for learning?

Just as teachers are called upon to differentiate instruction, so too should administrators strive to differentiate professional development offerings to the teachers in the early stages of their careers. A new hire with six years of experience and an earned masters degree does not want to spend his/her time in mandatory seminars and workshops four hours a month. He/she may need some of the workshops that are specific to the district and state standards and the school's demographics. That teacher may be the ideal person to lead a short-term study group of teachers interested in pursuing a master's degree.

Providing as much choice as possible to teachers in their own professional development can be a key to their retention. Distributing the learning over a five-year time frame may lessen the stress of being overwhelmed. Sometimes good professional development might mean a free two hours to talk with the mentor or small team of mentors about rearranging the classroom.

One of the rewards of working in higher education is the opportunity to attend conferences around the country and to network through those conferences. Can travel money be allocated to send teachers to conferences for learning and renewal? For teachers willing and able to pay for their own conference attendance, can personal leave time be granted? When teachers return from a conference or workshop they can lead discussions about their learning.

SUMMARY POINTS FOR SUCCESS

1. Ongoing professional development for teachers during their first five years may be critical to their retention.
2. Induction program offerings should be personalized with choices available for the content of what will be studied.
3. Administrators guide the induction program, but teachers themselves can lead seminars and professional learning communities.
4. Offerings must be timely, but can't take up too much time or teachers will become completely overwhelmed.
5. Induction offerings should help to build a collegial, supportive school culture.

Chapter Seven

Supportive Administration, Supervision, and Evaluation

In this district, you are either teaching students, or supporting those who do.
—Common saying among superintendents

If the saying above is as common as it seems, then those who are not directly teaching students should be directly supporting all teachers, and especially new hires. What does "support" mean? What do new hires seek as their support? How can administrators provide support and still evaluate teacher performance objectively to make decisions about rehiring or releasing faculty?

Writing about her first year as a principal, and working specifically with Millennial teachers, Barker (2015) wrote that new hires seek collaboration and value for the work that they do. In her words, "The staff needed more opportunities to work together and develop authentic relationships beyond meetings and trainings. If I had focused on building a family spirit, I would have created a better team." Barker then added, "Teachers will not stay in an environment where they do not feel valued" (p. 7).

Support is a concept, with different meanings for different teachers. For some, it means leaving them alone and letting them teach. For others, it means if they send a student to the office for disciplinary action, they expect the administrator to provide genuine disciplinary action and not to send the student back to the classroom in two minutes. Support may mean giving affirmative feedback and praise often and reassuring the teachers that they are doing good work in a challenging job. Support involves knowing the teachers, providing opportunities for their learning, and being positive about their work. Support is being collegial.

Glickman, Gordon, and Ross-Gordon (2001) wrote the following:

> A successful school like Progress Middle School is a collegial school—characterized by purposeful adult interactions about improving schoolwide teaching and learning. Professional respect is a by-product of discussing issues with candor, accepting disagreements as integral to change, and respecting the wisdom and care of all for arriving at educational decisions for students. (p. 5)

Support is shown through collegiality and through an administrator who creates the respectful, positive atmosphere in the school. Supportive administrators know who does what and how well they do it. Few things lower morale more quickly than when a principal rewards or rehires a weak or marginal teacher. Supportive administrators care about employees and demonstrate that care through genuine conversations and interactions with them.

Supportive administrators recognize that teachers have tough jobs. They don't belittle a new teacher whose students may have lower than average test scores; rather, they find a way to provide intervention strategies for reaching all students and provide more support teachers to the group of students. They certainly don't yell at their teachers when low standardized test scores are posted.

Supportive administrators are nice, not mean. Yes, the administrator must also make tough decisions, releasing those who are not doing their jobs well. Teachers-in-training learn that they must be assertive, not mean, when dealing with students. Administrators should learn the same lesson in their training with regard to working with teachers.

Considerable research points to the fact that Millennials want much positive feedback when they do something well, and they want that feedback often. This is in contrast to most district guidelines on supervision and evaluation, where a teacher is observed one to three times a year. After earning tenure, observation of a teacher may drop to once every third year. A common lament of new teachers may be, "I just wish my principal knew how hard I was working and could see my daily successes." How can supervision be more frequent and still be reasonably doable for busy administrators?

A simple suggestion is to build trust with teachers and ask them what is going well every week. A short conversation in the hallway before or after school provides the opportunity for a teacher to share his/her best moment of the week. Asking teachers this electronically may work well, as some teachers may want to share successes through e-mail.

After a few weeks, and in a trusting relationship, teachers will begin to confide challenges and make suggestions about what help they need. Glickman, Gordon, and Ross-Gordon (2001) call this the interpersonal skills base of the supervisor. "Supervisors must know how their own interpersonal behaviors affect individuals as well as groups of teachers and then study ranges of interpersonal behaviors that might be used to promote more positive and change-oriented relationships" (p. 11).

There are differences between observing a teacher and supervising one. Evaluation occurs as a result of supervision and other assessment measures. There should also be differences in the approach to supervising and evaluating a novice teacher and a veteran. "A delicate balance must be maintained between nurturing novice teachers to promote their personal well-being on the one hand, and nudging them to learn and improve their teaching performance on the other hand" (Nolan and Hoover, 2011, p. 85).

With regard to what new teachers want: they want to know how they will be supervised, and how that supervision contributes to their evaluation for reemployment. Make the district guidelines clear in the interview, in orientation, and again in the ongoing seminars for new hires. Train the mentor teachers regarding supervision and evaluation guidelines, so that they are providing the new hires with the same set of guidelines as the administrators.

SUPERVISION AND EVALUATION

"What would you do if you knew you couldn't fail?" is an old question often asked in motivational workshops. What would new hires do if they knew that there was a safety net to catch them if they did fail? Both district and individual school administrators need to develop the philosophy behind their supervision and evaluation systems, and to make that philosophy known to the teachers—in the interview, in orientation, and throughout the first years.

In the supervision of teachers' work, there is a time to be direct, a time to be indirect, and a time to be collegial. Consider the following examples:

Direct supervision and intervention needed

1. Teacher is repeatedly late to work. (Document each occurrence.)
2. Teacher is not teaching the mandated curriculum. (Document with copies of lesson plans.)
3. The classroom is overly noisy and teacher's students are misbehaving at lunch, on the playground, and in the hallways.
4. Students are not in their assigned classroom. Teacher allows students to wander in the halls and other school areas.
5. Teacher is not in the room, leaving students without supervision.
6. In an observation, the teacher is sarcastic and belittles students.

Indirect Supervision

1. Observer has enough data to ensure that the teacher is doing quite well and asks for the teacher's input on when to observe again.

2. Observer discusses ideas for growth with the teacher, listening to what the teacher wants to learn or change about the job.
3. Observer makes suggestions about having the teacher begin, or add to, their leadership roles.

Collegial Supervision

1. Observer discusses a lesson plan with the teacher and offers to plan together (a good role for a mentor).
2. Observer asks lots of questions about the lessons observed and why the teacher has chosen to teach with certain strategies.
3. Observer discusses a new textbook with the teacher and together they plan how to implement its use.
4. Observer and teacher discuss strategies to improve the behavior of a specific student.
5. Observer and teacher attend a workshop together and discuss implementation of what was learned.

Observations may be used by multiple people to support the new teacher. A mentor can, and should, be observing the new hire and working with him/her in a collegial manner. It can be valuable for a new hire to observe another new hire, as they have so much in common. In schools where instructional coaches are used, these coaches are another layer of observation. The supervisor who will eventually evaluate the new hire's needs to know the strengths and deficits of the hire well enough to know how direct to be with regard to supervision and following district guidelines.

The philosophy of supervision and of evaluation should be to support teachers to be as effective as possible in their classrooms. Effective teachers guide student learning and raise student achievement. Effective teachers need to be rehired and retained in classrooms.

Models for Observation

Clinical or collegial supervision

Both mentors and evaluators can use basic observational techniques to guide and evaluate teachers. Called "clinical" or "collegial" supervision by different authors, using a cycle of preconference, observation, and postconference has become a widely accepted practice for effective observations of teachers. In this style of observation, there are no "gotcha" observations where an observer arrives unannounced to critique, criticize, and list teacher deficits. Instead, there is a cycle of the preconference, the observation, and the postconference.

Noted for their work in the field of clinical supervision, Acheson and Gall (2003) purport the cyclical nature of observation. They stress that the supervisor must meet with the teacher and plan for scheduled observations, observe a lesson systematically and nonjudgmentally, record information related to objectives discussed together, and then meet with the teacher to analyze findings and interpret data. Together, the teacher and the supervisor "reach decisions about the next steps" (p. 9).

There is much value in talking with a teacher to plan observations. In this the supervisor learns what the teacher views as strengths and weaknesses. Asking the teacher what he/she wants the observer to watch for, and to plan how to record data that can be reviewed, provides teacher buy-in to the entire process. (See appendix 7.1 for a template for observation preconferences.)

Will teachers, especially new hires, be honest about the instructional strategies, student behavior issues, and overall workings of their classes when their administrators use preconferences for planned observations? The answer to this question depends on the trust levels built during the orientation sessions, the work with mentors, the ongoing induction programs, and the interpersonal relationship built with the administrator conducting the observation.

Many student teachers are used to being observed with clinical/collegial supervision, and would be surprised by another approach. Other new hires may be totally overwhelmed by having to provide input into the objectives of their own observations. Again, there is always a time to be direct, a time to be indirect, and a time to be collegial with each new hire. Explaining the observation model, and using it consistently, is the key to its success.

A veteran teacher once said that her supervisor's observations and evaluations were only as valid as the evaluator's skill set for observing and evaluating. There is certainly merit to this statement. An observer must know what good teaching looks like, what instructional strategies work for certain grades and subjects, and what indicates genuine student engagement.

A strong observer/supervisor knows in advance what to look for in the classroom, as that was the purpose of conducting a preconference. The observer arrives on time, enters unobtrusively, and is truly an observer, not getting involved in the teaching or management of the class. Data should be gathered as objectively as possible, using seating charts to mark student engagement, tallying numbers of questions asked and answered by students, and teacher movement. Specific strategies for gathering data follow:

1. Have the teacher provide a seating chart. Using the chart, mark with lines and directional arrows the teacher's movements. This may be especially helpful if observing a teacher supervising group work. Look for:

- movement around the room; not overlooking any group of students
- ability of students to see the teacher and the visuals in class as the student moves

2. Have the teacher provide a seating chart with males and females identified. Mark each time (tally mark) the teacher interacts with each student. Does the teacher call on each gender equally? Does the teacher wait longer for students of one gender than the other to answer questions?
3. On a seating chart provided by the teacher, have the teacher mark students with regard to general achievement (high, medium, low). While observing, watch to see if the teacher calls upon all students equally. (Put tally marks by each student's seat on chart.) Also, mark a plus when the teacher provides praise to a student. Does the teacher apply appropriate praise equally?
4. For a teacher seeking help with classroom management issues, use a seating chart to mark student misbehaviors. For example, mark each time a student:

- speaks or blurts out without permission
- is out of their assigned seat
- talks with another student
- sleeps or appears to pay no attention
- does not do what the teacher has instructed

A strong observer also knows what an effective lesson looks like. He/she looks for introductions, presentations, times for student practice, and conclusions. A sample follows:

1. Focus/review or introduction is evident.
2. New material was presented in a clear manner.
3. Visuals supported lecture/presentation of material.
4. Students had opportunities to apply/practice material.
5. Instructor's voice was understandable. Instructor's tone with students was supportive (no sarcasm, etc.).
6. Was there evidence of student engagement (asking questions, not texting, etc.)?
7. Conclusion or review was evident.
8. Instructor had clear goals and objectives and those were met.

Recording verbatim statements and questions is important for judging the level of academics as well as the tone set by the teacher. The use of video recording allows the teacher and the observer to review the class together, discussing relevant points. Writing out the exact words used by the teacher and the students provides ample material for review and discussion in the postconference. (See appendix 7.2 for a guide on taking verbatim notes.)

From my own experiences supervising preservice and in-service teachers, I can share that recordings and verbatim notes have yielded the following surprises to the teachers observed:

1. The teacher had no idea that she said "you guys" continually throughout her teaching.
2. The teacher was surprised that she called on males more than twice as much as females to answer questions. "Well," she said, "they will blurt out if I don't call on them."
3. The teacher did not realize that she taught the material incorrectly, mixing up the names of the generals in the Civil War.
4. The teacher did not know the meaning of a word in Spanish, so he made one up. "They are only students, they won't know the difference," he said in the postconference.
5. The teacher said that he simply did not hear the student swear at him.
6. The teacher said that he didn't know that one student never opened the book, answered a question, copied a note from the board, or wrote on the worksheet.
7. The teacher never called on a single student in the back of the room to her left.

These examples point to the fact that novice teachers are intent on what they are doing and getting through their lesson plan. On the other hand, I have completed many observations where the teacher thought their lesson was OK, or even weak, when it was outstanding. Gathering data and sharing it allows teachers to not only grow on targeted objectives, but to also improve on their self-reflection.

Guiding the teacher to reflect upon practice is one goal of having observation postconferences and having them as soon as possible after the observation. (See appendix 7.3.) Teachers will want some feedback as the observer leaves the room, yet this is not the time to say anything to the teacher, especially in front of students.

Students in the room often ask how their teacher is doing or if the observer will give the teacher a high grade. Elementary students sometimes want to provide feedback to the observer, telling him/her that the teacher is "the best in the world" or that "we love her." Older students rarely give this type of feedback, but may be prone to say, "He is awesome," or "Don't fire her—we are learning new stuff."

Keeping with the philosophy of supporting teachers through observations and striving to get teachers to reflect on their practice, a starting point for the observation postconference is to ask the teacher how he/she thought the lesson went, and if he/she accomplished the stated goals and objectives for the lesson.

While some teachers will overrate their performance, others will underrate it, especially at the beginning of use of this model of observation. Hopefully, as the process continues, all teachers will become more adept at reviewing their own practice. This is critically necessary, as teachers will work most of their careers in classrooms without the immediate supervisor present.

In an observation postconference, the observer and the teacher look at the information (data) gathered, discuss it, draw conclusions, and plan for changes or improvements. (See appendix 7.3 for a template of managing an observation postconference.) Postconferences end with plans for the next observation cycle. Time should be allowed for the teacher to ask other questions about teaching, final evaluations, or whatever needs to be asked.

How long should pre- and post-observation conferences be? Authors vary in their answer to this question, but conferences may take twenty to thirty minutes. Where does the mentor, or the evaluator, have such time? It is a valid question, especially if the observer is to see multiple classes throughout the year. One administrator had "virtual" preconferences by asking the questions through e-mail. Another said that she limited her conferences to ten minutes to keep them from becoming gripe sessions.

While the actual number of minutes for a conference may vary, it is the conversation that matters. Millennials seek feedback—often, and in a positive manner. They want to talk about their teaching, to collaborate, and to try new ideas. The conferences before and after observations build a level of collegiality and trust needed to build the positive school culture.

The model of clinical/collegial supervision has been researched for decades and has shown results of improving teacher effectiveness. (See, for example, Acheson and Gall, 2003.) Keeping the philosophy of supporting teachers and increasing their effectiveness through observations is a key to effective teacher retention.

Walk-through observations

Walk-through observations are a blend of observation and evaluation that are often used in the supervision of teachers. Historically, principals often gleaned information about a teacher and his/her work simply by walking by a classroom. Principals could tell if the room was quiet, with students working at desks, or if the room was noisy, with students wandering around. However, this is not enough to actually evaluate student engagement or a teacher's level of planning and instruction.

Walk-through evaluations are of most value when they have a purpose. One example is walking through the classroom during the first few weeks of the year to check on desk arrangements, the posting of emergency and management plans, and overall organization of the room. (See appendix 7.4 for a checklist.) Of course, teachers should see this checklist during orientation and know that they will receive a walk-through visit at some point in the first three weeks of the school year.

Because "Frequent snapshots of a teacher's behaviors and interactions give the principal a better chance of collecting valid data" (DiPaola and Hoy, 2008, p. 119), there should be multiple walk-throughs, at different times, to provide some validity to the process. When first implemented, teachers are generally apprehensive, but become less so as the walk-through process becomes more routine.

Documentation is important. The observer should record the time, specific teacher and student behaviors observed, and the organization of the room. (See appendix 7.5.) Comments should be observable, without assessment or opinion. For example, "Teacher seated at desk from 10:12 to 10:17" and not, "Teacher never moves from desk during observation. Is she/he tired?"

Just as with clinical observations, teachers will want feedback from the walk-through observation. Plan when and how to provide that feedback. Teachers should get a copy of the notes taken, and should receive the notes in a reasonable amount of time. For a positive walk-through, leaving the notes in the teacher's mailbox may be enough. For a more negative walk-through, where issues were obvious, providing the copy of notes with a conversation may be better.

Administrators who use walk-through evaluations tend to look for trends. If the teacher is seated at his/her desk in a first-grade classroom every time that the principal walks through, that may be a trend that merits discussion. If students are loud and talkative in each observation, a follow-up conversation or longer observation may be needed. Walk-through visits are a more difficult to interpret, as the observer does not have the advantage of a pre-observation conference to learn about context. Savvy observers will not judge all behaviors they see without asking the teacher for some background context.

In some school districts, administrators are asked to do only walk-through observations or only more traditional classroom visits. The combination of a series of walk-through visits and two to three clinical supervision-style observations will give a clearer picture of the teacher's work. Using the data from a variety of observations is useful when completing the teacher's summative evaluation for the year and for re-employment.

EVALUATION OF TEACHERS

The accountability movement has bound administrators to strict standards with regard to teacher evaluation. While teacher observations have long been a part of teacher evaluation, students' test scores, students' evaluations of their teachers, and parents' evaluations are often added to the overall evaluation process. Portfolio assessment may be used as a part of a final teacher evaluation, where the teacher must provide student work samples and proof of teaching that has impacted student learning. Professional companies have joined the teacher evaluation bandwagon, with assessments such as edTPA. (See www.edtpa.com.)

DiPaola and Hoy wrote that "a credible evaluation is based on the premise that both evaluators and those they evaluate know and understand all the elements of the job, the performance expectations, and how their performance will be assessed" (2008, p. 153). Evaluations need to be completed based on observable data and valid indicators. As more and more school districts include student and parent surveys in final teacher evaluations, it is important to consider the reliability and validity of those surveys.

The use of student achievement data in teacher evaluations is controversial. While it has been said that "the use of student achievement data ensures that evaluations hold teachers accountable while providing feedback that can be used to help teachers improve their effectiveness" (DiPaola and Hoy, 2008, p. 158), there are significant concerns over the use of students' test scores as an evaluation of the teacher. Test scores may be significantly lower depending on the native language of students in the class or the socioeconomic demographics of the school.

Very few administrators have to create their own teacher evaluation forms, as districts seek consistency in teacher evaluations. The data gathered from all observations, student achievement, and sources such as parent and student surveys should be reviewed. Exit interviews with the teacher at the end of a school year can provide more information. Consider asking the teacher the following (in a conversation, or as a survey) before completion of the final evaluation document:

1. What were the highlights of this school year for you?
2. Describe the overall achievement of your students this year. How do you know that this was their achievement level?
3. Are you pleased with the student achievement this year?
4. What did you do differently this year than in the past? Why?
5. What would you like to see changed for next year in our school?
6. What would you like to learn or improve upon next year?

It is important to only use valid data in teacher evaluation. What should NOT be used?

- Do not rely on the comments of one or two parents to evaluate a teacher. Observe the teacher, follow the mandated evaluation criteria, and look at all the data.
- Do not rely on a few student comments to gain a picture of the teacher's work. A fifteen-year old who doesn't want to take notes in class or do homework may not be the best source for teacher evaluation.
- Be cautious of relying on the comments of other teachers with regard to the evaluation of a teacher. Some teachers themselves do not see the big picture, or may feel intimidated by a new hire and their comments may not be objective ones.
- Be cautious of rumors about a teacher. Do not evaluate a teacher's performance based on hearsay.

Remediation and Release of Teachers

Even with all of the support systems in place to help teachers, some teachers will not perform up to standards. Low-performing teachers must be identified immediately, as student learning will suffer with a weak teacher. Follow the district protocol to provide an intervention to help the teacher with a specific issue, and create a plan to remediate a deficit in training or experience. In the worst-case scenario, follow the district guidelines for release of the teacher and nonrenewal of a contract.

Some general guidelines for teacher remediation and release include:

1. Begin conversations about low performance as soon as that performance is noted. Alert the teacher verbally and in writing about what needs to change. For example:

   - You must be in the classroom by 7:45 a.m. You will receive a written notification each time you are late, and may be released at any time for continued tardiness.
   - On Wednesday, September 10, five of your students were unsupervised for more than forty minutes. They must remain in your room under your supervision.

2. Follow all district guidelines for remediation and nonrenewal of contract. Inform the human resources office and/or superintendent as soon as the issues arise. Keep all informed.
3. Depending on the state, the teachers' association/union may be involved in the issue of a teacher's remediation or release from a position. Know the union guidelines and follow them. Keep the union representative apprised of all issues from the beginning.

4. Strive to stem gossip about teachers' performance in general and about a specific teacher's issues. If asked by a teacher about another teacher, it is often best to say, "I am aware of issues and am following district protocol. As you know, there are strict confidentiality issues regarding evaluation and employment."

Teachers who are not fulfilling their job responsibilities can, and should, be released, even if they are tenured. Following due process and district guidelines is the only way to make that happen.

SUMMARY POINTS FOR SUCCESS

1. An evaluator must see a teacher in the classroom to actually evaluate the quality of his/her teaching. Walk-through observations, combined with longer, planned observations, provide a picture of the teacher's work.
2. When evaluating a teacher, much data must be gathered from multiple sources. Consider the data from observations, student achievement, and student or parent surveys, but never hearsay or gossip.
3. Making today's new hires, especially Millennials, feel supported in their work is critical in retaining them in the teaching force. Support comes from professional conversations, positive feedback, and the creation of a collegial work environment.
4. The building principal is not the only one who can provide support. Trained mentors can use collegial/clinical observation methods to observe and provide feedback to teachers that is supportive without being part of their final evaluation.
5. A teacher's evaluation may only be as valid as the evaluator's training and expertise in evaluation. A strong evaluator knows best practice in teaching, knows how to observe, and knows how to gather data for a final evaluation.

Chapter Eight

Developing Teacher Leaders

> In my professional opinion, we have only begun to explore the possibilities of teacher leadership.
>
> —Bond (2015, p. 2)

All educators know teachers who want to "fly under the radar" and not become involved in anything that involves extra hours, work, or responsibilities. "Just let me teach in my room" may be their mantra. However, are these the teachers the school administrators want to retain for a lifetime career?

The opposite of the under-the-radar teacher may be the teacher leader. Barth (2001) wrote:

> Teachers who become leaders experience personal and professional satisfaction, a reduction in isolation, a sense of instrumentality, and new learnings—all of which spill over into their teaching. As school-based reformers, these teachers become owners and investors in the school, rather than mere tenants. (p. 443)

Hargreaves (2015) wrote, "Leadership is at its best when it is distributed throughout the workplace, a classroom, or a school" (p. x). He continued with the following:

> Teacher leadership is, at one level, an inescapable reality. All teachers already are leaders of students, of people large and small. By design or default, teachers also are leaders of change, whether they promote it, support it, resist it, or ignore it. The question is, therefore, not whether teacher leadership is needed, but whether this leadership can and should extend in deliberate and positive ways. (2015, p. x)

ROLES OF TEACHER LEADERS

Teacher leadership roles mirror the components of teachers' jobs—curriculum, instruction, assessment, and classroom management. Then, leadership roles go beyond the classroom to include work with hiring, mentoring, and professional development of their colleagues. What are some typical roles for teacher leaders?

1. Curriculum

    • Teachers can choose books, materials, and technology. When teachers have a voice in the materials and resources they use, they are much more apt to use them.
    • As the curriculum standards change, grade-level leaders can be trained off-site and return to train their colleagues.
    • Teacher leaders can observe the implementation and assessment of curriculum with each other, by grade and subject.
    • Teachers can write curriculum maps and scope and sequence charts for curriculum implementation.
    • Instruction
    • Teachers can share strategies formally in seminars/workshops and through planned discussions.
    • Teachers can observe each other to learn best practice.
    • A teacher leader may become an instructional coach for a specific area, such as math or literacy.
    • Teachers can be leaders in the implementation of new technology.

2. Assessment

    • Teachers can lead test review or standardized test–preparation sessions.
    • Teachers can grade assignments together, improving reliability and validity of individual assessments.
    • Teachers can review test results together, looking for areas of improvement.

3. Classroom management

    • Teachers should be the leaders in the development or updating of the school-wide management plan.
    • Teachers can train others in the creation of a usable classroom management plan.

- Teachers can receive training in violence prevention and share with their grade or subject-level colleagues.

4. Hiring

- Teachers, with training, can serve as interviewers of new teacher candidates.
- Teachers can serve in writing specific job descriptions for position openings.
- Teachers can open their classrooms for a candidate to teach a model, or mini-lesson, to students and also provide input to administrators about that lesson.

5. Mentoring

- Serving as a mentor to a new teacher is a leadership role. Mentors must be trained.
- After mentoring new mentors, a teacher can become a leader in mentor training.
- A mentor can be the facilitator of an ongoing mentor discussion/ support group.
- A teacher can evaluate a mentor program, gathering surveys from all mentors and compiling the data.

6. Social activities

- Many teachers revel in planning social events. This may be a way for some to lead who do not wish to be involved in other leadership roles.

7. Professional development seminar leaders

- Teachers can plan professional development offerings for the faculty, beginning with surveys and needs assessments of topics.
- Teachers can share what they have learned in their own graduate courses as professional development. One idea: Have a panel of teachers who have recently completed their master's degrees share the issues involved in getting a master's degree. (See appendix 8.1 for specifics.)
- Teachers make great leaders of book studies and professional learning communities.

8. School environment

- One principal felt that teachers always complained when he decided if it was warm enough for outside recess. He asked for volunteers and a three-person weather recess committee made the decision. This small leadership role was a big step in building a better relationship between faculty and the principal.
- Teachers can be involved in building improvement decisions. For some teachers, choosing the color for the paint in their room is a big deal.
- Using a principal's advisory committee has value. In some districts this is mandated by the union, and in others the teachers vote for the committee each new school year. The committee generates ideas when needed, and provides feedback to a principal who may not otherwise have this means of communication with faculty.

9. Public relations

- Teachers are subject-matter experts and many appreciate when their expertise is shared. Teachers can speak at Rotary Club meetings and similar community events. They can, and should, represent the school in a very positive light.
- Serving as a liaison to the school's parent organization (PTA or PTO) is a valuable leadership role.
- Teachers can lead their students in community events. One French teacher had her students go Christmas caroling on the downtown square, with all the songs in French, of course.
- Service learning and volunteer efforts are increasingly common. Teachers often lead community food drives and similar projects.

10. Professional association/union roles

- Teachers' professional associations/unions offer leadership training for teachers, which can be very valuable.
- Encouraging teachers to remain active in their professional associations, such as Kappa Delta Pi, the international honor society for teachers, provides another venue for teachers to collaborate outside of the district and to have rewarding leadership roles. All teachers should maintain memberships in subject-matter professional associations, such as the International Reading Association or the National Council of Teachers of English, and there are associations for every subject field. For some teachers, attendance at an annual conference is exactly the positive reward needed to combat burnout.

11. Extracurricular/cocurricular duties

- Coaches hold leadership roles that also propel them into the public relations spotlight. For those who love coaching, this is the retention tool that keeps them in teaching.
- Other roles might be sponsoring the school newspaper, school plays, honor society, or volunteer events.
- Leading an after-school program or a summer school program provides the "something extra" that some teachers seek.

Promoting Teacher Leaders

Some administrators use the word "let" and think that is promoting teacher leadership. "I'll let the teachers decide how to do that," or "I'll let the teachers give some input" are examples. In fact, it would be better to remove the word "let" from all administrators' vocabulary and speech patterns! Better verbs are "encourage," "invite," "ask," and "seek input." Administrators who believe in distributed leadership endorse the development of teacher leaders. They see the value of having teachers who do more than just teach. These teacher leaders help to transform the school environments and teaching itself.

How does one promote teacher leadership and where does it start? Bond's research (2011) indicates that leadership begins in the teacher education preparation program. He calls on colleges to prepare students and student teachers for leadership roles throughout their teacher preparation programs. When a college offers leadership opportunities to students, the development of skills begins.

Consider asking job candidates about their previous leadership roles. Using the behavior-based questioning model, the questions would be worded as follows:

- Tell us about any leadership roles you have held while in college (or high school).
- Describe how you have led a classroom activity that involved planning and working with other teachers.

Remembering that behavior-based interviewing is steeped in the premise that past behavior is the best predictor of future performance, it follows that a new hire who had some leadership experience before teaching will be more likely to seek leadership opportunities when hired. When hiring, consider a candidate who organized social events in the dorm or who held an officer's position in a student organization. Kappa Delta Pi, the international honor society for educators, has hundreds of campus chapters and offers leadership training and opportunities for members. These teacher education students are primed to be leaders in the schools that hire them.

The idea of teacher leadership meshes well with the characterization of today's Millennial employees. Even as new hires, this generation of teachers wants a voice and wants to be heard. They want to improve and transform classrooms and teaching.

What are some of the simplest roles for teacher leaders? Barth (2001) includes simply leading by example as a leadership role. Some teachers are leaders by their enthusiasm and persistence with work. They lead by letting others observe their model lessons and sharing their resources.

Membership on committees may be seen as leadership, even when one doesn't chair the committee. Providing input on issues and attending meetings leads to the opportunity of leading. In essence, being an involved teacher who always acts professionally is perhaps a first step to leadership.

If the value of teacher leadership is so highly rated, why isn't this the norm in schools? Time is always a factor and new hires are operating in survival mode. The key is finding the right opportunity for the teacher at the right time. It really doesn't help to always ask the same teachers to lead initiatives. One teacher, when asked to write a large portion of her school's accreditation report quipped, "I feel awful that I can't say no. I just accept the extra work and move on." That approach generally leads a strong teacher to move to another school, where he/she isn't asked to do everything.

Another pitfall is having some teachers take over too many administrative duties. This may create an atmosphere of distrust by colleagues. If teachers are completing internships or graduate degrees in administration, they will take on supervised administrative duties in a formal way, and that may ease the tension of a teacher assuming a quasi-administrative job. The success to this type of internship or project lies with the training and supervision by the administrator. A long-term positive outcome of embedding teacher leadership into the school culture is growing one's own administrators, and there is a shortage of school administrators in many areas of the United States.

Teacher Leaders in Professional Learning Communities (PLCs)

There are many models of teacher PLCs. While some are as simple as choosing a book to read for a group of like-minded teachers, other PLCs conduct action research or delve into important school-wide problems and issues.

Consider the following guidelines:

1. What model for a professional learning community will be used? Is there a need to have a faculty-wide discussion/orientation about the PLCs?

2. What need does the establishment of learning communities fill? There is no need to burden teachers with attending a learning community just for the sake of checking it off on an accreditation checklist.
3. Ask teachers to define their professional development need that could be fulfilled by participation in a PLC. (Consider student behavior, standardized test scores, implementation of a new teacher evaluation system, etc.)
4. What are the intended outcomes of the learning? Will research be conducted? Will a study group provide recommendations to the administration or faculty?
5. Who will be invited to lead the groups and how will they receive training?
6. How will the groups be evaluated on their work?
7. How will time be found for the work? Will teachers receive any other perks or remuneration?

Of course, all administrators make parameters for teacher leaders within a school. Having clarity for the roles of mentor teachers, lead teachers, instructional coaches, and those who lead professional learning communities enhances the chance for success of the leaders, as well as for the collegiality established. Much of the success for teacher leadership lies within the quality of the school culture. There is so much work to be done in schools that shared leadership is a necessity.

SUMMARY POINTS FOR SUCCESS

1. The value of encouraging teachers to assume leadership positions is well established through research.
2. Many levels of teacher leadership are available, ranging from simply being the teacher who shares great ideas to being the teacher who leads a professional learning community that conducts research.
3. New hires who assumed leadership roles as college students will probably seek similar roles when hired.
4. One key for encouraging teachers to take advantage of leadership opportunities is to know when to suggest and invite them to do so.
5. While administrators do provide oversight of teachers in quasi-administrative leadership roles, strong administrators see the value of shared leadership.
6. Growing one's own administrators can be a result of providing teacher leadership roles in a school and district.

Chapter Nine

An Improved Workplace for Teachers

Professional culture has always had an impact on teachers' perspectives, practices, and beliefs.

—Hargreaves (2015, p. xi)

Much research exists on schools that are supportive of new teachers. The work of Susan Moore Johnson and The Project on the Next Generation of Teachers (2004) found the following:

Some schools are organized to support new teachers in succeeding with their students. These schools not only celebrate learning and promote hard work but also provide teachers and students with the infrastructure needed to work together productively. They organize time and space so that teachers are well connected with regular opportunities to exchange ideas and information. (p. 91)

Some of the infrastructure pointed out by Moore Johnson and that of her research team include:

- administrators who are responsive to teachers' needs
- administrators who know their faculty members and make appropriate assignments for them
- administrators who have appropriate personal relationships with faculty members and use appropriate interpersonal communications
- experienced faculty members who observe and consult with new hires
- genuinely supportive colleagues
- sufficient supplies and equipment for teaching
- school-wide discipline expectations/plans that are supported

- support services for students that meet student needs (counseling, tutoring, etc.)

What is professional culture and how is it defined? Moore Johnson and The Project on the Next Generation of Teachers (2004) wrote:

> Professional culture is the blend of values, norms, and modes of professional practice that develops among teachers in a school. The professional culture of a school has an enormous impact on new teachers, since they look toward their colleagues for signals about how best to do good work. Professional culture can be school-wide, or it can exist in subunits within the school, such as departments, grade-level teams, or clusters . . . . Indeed, the quality of new teachers' interactions with their colleagues may determine their success as teachers. (p. 140)

As mentioned earlier in this book, some administrators say that cash and culture are the two factors that retain teachers—especially effective teachers. Gruenert and Whitaker (2015) wrote, "When teachers feel they are making a contribution to their school, they enjoy their work more and accomplish far more than what any merit pay can yield" (p. 71).

Hancock and Scherff (2010) wrote that teachers leave schools because of lack of planning time, a too-heavy workload, a too-low salary, student behavior issues, and a lack of influence over policies in schools (p. 329). Some of these issues are ones that can be addressed by climate and culture changes, as well as comprehensive school improvement.

SCHOOL CLIMATE

Just how do administrators get an objective look at the school climate and the school as a workplace? Much of the data gathering to assess the workplace may come as a school participates in state and regional accreditation processes. Accreditation reviews include self-studies, and a self-study can reveal much about the strengths and weaknesses of a school. Consider the following:

1. What are the retention rates for teachers? Who is leaving? Where are they going?
2. Look at discipline referrals and student suspensions. Are the numbers constant, increasing, or decreasing?
3. What is the number of police calls to the school? Why were they needed?
4. What do standardized test scores indicate about student achievement?

5. What are attendance rates at parent events? How active is the parent/teacher association?
6. Ask teachers for their "needs" and "wishes" list. Take action on as many issues as possible. (See appendix 9.1.)
7. Ask for parent input about the school. Consider a parent survey. (See appendix 9.2.)
8. Walk through the building looking at facilities with a team of teachers. What needs painting? Cleaning? Maintenance?
9. Are there areas of the school in need of enhanced security?
10. Is there space for teachers to work outside of their classrooms?
11. Use "stay" interviews or surveys. These are conducted with veteran teachers who are effective and who can provide insight into why they remained in the school and in the teaching profession. (See below and appendix 9.3.)

Perhaps this can be a group interview, led by a veteran teacher or administrator. Consider some of the following questions for the face-to-face interview:

1. Our records indicate that you have been here x years. Why have you chosen to stay in this school for that amount of time?
2. How do you feel supported now in your role as a teacher?
3. How did you find support as a beginning teacher at this school?
4. Which in-service programs have been most beneficial to you?
5. What social events have you found to be supportive?
6. How do you see your future at the school?
7. What supports would you like to see implemented for all teachers?
8. What supports would you like to see improved for new hires?

When teachers or parents are asked for input, the results should be shared in a timely manner. After sharing the results, an action plan should be put in place for school improvement. After implementation, further assessments should be undertaken. It is an ongoing cycle.

One Specific Case: Improving Support for Management and Discipline

Issues of classroom management and dealing with students' behavioral issues remain as constant sources of teacher frustration and burnout. Often, teachers leave a school and take a teaching job in another school because, "The kids are better behaved and the administration sets the expectations high for behavior." Other teachers leave the profession for other jobs because, "The kids are just terrible." While these are paraphrases of what I have personally heard from dozens of teachers, they may be highly indicative of overall teacher sentiment.

What can administrators do to make the school's environment one supportive of good student behavior? How can administrators support teachers with regard to managing student behavior and creating well-managed classrooms? Administrators need to know the knowledge base of classroom management and discipline. They need updated training on management strategies that work and how to implement them. Administrators need to read the current research, find the best guidebooks, and then disseminate this information to groups of teachers for study and implementation.

Step 1: Make classroom management and student behavior a yearlong priority. Have all teachers read a series of articles or a book on effective classroom management during the spring semester before the new school year.

Step 2: Devote professional development time to guided discussions on improved classroom management. Have teachers lead the discussion.

Step 3: Get teacher input on the school's guidelines. Update the discipline policies. Clarify what the administrators can and can't do.

Step 4: Have a team of teachers and administrators walk through each classroom before the school year starts to look at seating arrangements, posted management plans with rules, and procedures. Use a four-step approach to management at the classroom level. (See appendix 9.4.)

Step 5: Assess the process of student behavior and discipline on an ongoing basis.

Supporting Instruction

An Australian study of work-environment issues and teacher burnout (Goddard, O'Brien, and Goddard, 2006) indicates that, "Work environments that were rated low in their ability to support innovative teaching were consistently associated with significant increases in burnout levels" (p. 868). Teachers seek empowerment in their instructional roles and independence from using a scripted curriculum.

How does the building administrator support instruction? First, the building principal needs to be aware of best practice, and then s/he needs the knowledge of how to guide and instruct adult learners in pedagogy. As Trachtman and Cooper (2010) wrote, principals have to become master teachers again. One way to lead instruction is to have a simplified plan for guiding and evaluating the teachers' instruction. Consider the following four-step plan for guiding instruction. When an observation evidences weak planning or teaching, share this as remediation to the teacher, as well. (See appendix 9.5.)

Step 1: A good lesson has a focus. A focus hooks students' attention, while also reviewing material and providing a rationale for the lesson. A focus may direct students to an objective, based on mandated standards, but a good lesson does not start with "Open your books to page 67."

Step 2: There must be material in a lesson. Teachers present material and also use visuals and technology to introduce the information. The material in a lesson has to be organized, with care taken to ensure that mandated curriculum is being taught. Material has to developmentally appropriate.

Step 3: Students must interact with the material being taught. This application step involves active learning. There should be tasks for students to do. The way to keep students on-task is to have tasks where they apply their learning. The presentation of new material and the application of the material should be woven together. Today's students can't apply their learning if they don't practice applications frequently in class.

Step 4: Lessons need to end with a planned conclusion. Assessments of learning need to take place with every lesson. A short, formative assessment gives the teacher feedback and a starting place for the next lesson.

Some of the mandated observation policies for the evaluation of instruction are so detailed, and so esoteric, that teachers don't know how to plan for instruction. When an administrator can simplify basic lesson planning to four steps, it guides teachers to plan for instruction. Watching for four basic steps guides administrators in their observations, as well.

Trachtman and Cooper's research indicates, "Most teachers attributed growth to assistance from colleagues rather than support from their principals" (2010, p. 51). Can supportive instruction be a shared leadership duty, with mentors and coaches involved in guiding teachers' instructional practices? The answer is a resounding yes, and this may be the only way to truly provide instructional guidance, as grade level and subject matter instructional practices vary widely.

Good Colleagues/Peer Support

If the number one reason that anyone leaves a job is that he/she doesn't feel supported by a boss, is the number two reason for leaving that an employee can't get along with co-workers, or finds them to be nonsupportive? It's a hypothetical question, but research does point to peer support as a factor in teacher retention (Hancock & Scherff, 2010).

What can be done to create a school climate where teachers respect and support each other? Should teacher education programs teach units on working with colleagues? In a teacher education program, students are generally prepared for team teaching. Student teaching is also the time when a preservice teacher must cooperate with an assigned teacher for an entire semester.

Behavior-based interview questions can ascertain a candidate's past experience working with others. Consider the following questions for inclusion in an interview:

1. Describe a time when you planned a lesson with another person.
2. Describe your student teaching experience. Specifically, how did you and your teacher work together?
3. (For teachers with experience) Tell about a time when you planned or worked with other teachers to create materials or teach lessons together.
4. Tell about a time you felt supported by other students in your college classes or supported by fellow teachers in a school.

When interviewing candidates, red flags may appear as indicators of a candidate's inability to get along with future colleagues. A candidate who complains that he/she had the worst student teaching supervisor will probably be the new hire who complains about the assigned mentor or peer coach.

To be supported by colleagues, a teacher must be a supportive colleague. Teachers become supportive and collegial when they have to time to work together. Whenever possible, block time for grade-level meetings and planning.

Unfortunately, some teachers continue teaching after experiencing burnout. Their low morale can have an effect on new hires. I vividly remember a veteran teacher telling me that I should leave the school and the teaching profession while I was still young enough to get another job. This teacher was counting the days (although it was years) to his own retirement. Teachers with low morale need an intervention themselves, so that they don't bring down other faculty members. In today's world of high-stakes teacher accountability, this teacher would have probably been asked to resign, or required to complete a significant retraining intervention.

New hires, especially Millennials, seek fairness in teaching assignments, evaluations, and the treatment of all employees. New hires resent the special treatment of one teacher over others. If all teachers are to be at work at 7:45 a.m. and everyone knows who rolls in at about 8 a.m. without a reprimand or intervention, morale is hurt. Teachers are like the students in a classroom. They want fairness and they see inequality very quickly.

Teaching awards are an interesting area of teacher morale. Yes, publicly recognizing the work of a teacher can be very rewarding to that teacher. A teacher who is named a district teacher-of-the-year, and who then serves as a spokesperson for the district, may become the best cheerleader for the school, its teachers, and the district.

Some award-winning teachers have a year off from their classrooms to mentor others, recruit new hires, and work closely with administration on special duties. This is a way to recruit new administrators, too. Other teachers just want a plaque for the wall with no additional duties.

How are teacher awards determined? Is there a best way to publicly recognize teachers' work as a retention tool? Some considerations include:

1. Have consistent guidelines for teacher recognition and always use the guidelines.
2. When possible, have teachers provide some input on awards. Past recipients of an award may constitute the committee that makes recommendations for future award winners.
3. Administrators need to know their teachers' work well enough to know who is really doing the best teaching, and who is just talking about doing the best teaching.
4. Thank all teachers in a timely, and frequent, manner. Today's Millennial workers see instant, positive feedback, and they seek it often.
5. It should go without saying that the administrator can't just nominate his/her friends for the awards.

TEACHER VOICE AND INPUT

There is an old saying about teachers and their abilities to do things. Paraphrased, it's something like, "It's too bad that the people who could run the world are busy teaching school." Sometimes the saying is "It's too bad that the people who should be president (or in Congress) are busy teaching school." Yes, many teachers do have a strong sense of efficacy. I personally believe that I could line people up and get them on a plane with my teaching skills far better than most airport gate agents.

How can teacher input (voice) be utilized for improvement of the school as a workplace? How can voice be used to support collegiality and retention? The following are some considerations:

1. In some states, the teachers' unions and professional associations are the collective voice for teachers. These groups have negotiated the areas where teacher input must be gathered and used. Follow the union and association guidelines. Work collaboratively with the associations' leaders.
2. When teachers are surveyed for their input, provide feedback to the teachers about the survey results. Electronic programs make surveys a quick and inexpensive way to get feedback. Consider the simplest of

surveys, such as questions about homecoming or any event. (See appendix 9.6.)

3. Provide opportunities for voting, such as voting on dates for breaks on a calendar. Create three possible calendars, all of which meet district mandates, and have teachers decide which works best for them.

4. Always have teachers evaluate professional development offerings. This includes professional learning groups, book studies, and committee meetings.

5. Some teachers want to give input on what their administrators consider small details. In one school, teachers complained about the principal's guidelines for when students could go outside at recess. A committee was formed and a group of teachers then determined which days had acceptable weather for outdoor recess.

For an example of what not to do, consider the following:

When a school is asked to accept student teachers from a neighboring university, the principal picks the teachers for the assignments and delivers the list to the whole faculty in a meeting. Teachers were not consulted. One teacher has an ill parent and feels that she just can't take on "one more thing" this school year. Yet, she knows the principal doesn't like teachers to complain or request changes. This lowers teacher morale. Assigning a student teacher to a weak teacher in hopes that the student teacher will help the children learn more is also a terrible idea, but a situation that happens frequently.

Why use teacher input for decisions? Why seek their input at all? It is not about simply appeasing teachers. Teachers are on the front lines with the students. They know when students are too tired to learn or when students have no appropriate clothing for outdoor recess. Good, effective teachers are advocates for their students and their colleagues.

What about complaints and teacher morale? Has anyone determined a best way to stop teachers from complaining? New hires often hear the complaints and immediately lament having taken the job, even if they had perceived this as their dream job. It is a given that someone will always complain. However, there are better and worse ways to complain.

Some administrators allow negative leaders to complain and joke as class clowns in faculty meetings. Just as when a student becomes a class clown, a one-on-one personal conference with a faculty member may be a way to curb public negativity. While this book stresses supportive administration to retain teachers, there are times when an administrator must reprimand and curtail certain teacher behaviors. Do so according to district policy. Of course, not all teachers should be retained. The nonrenewal of a contract for certain teachers may actually raise morale of those remaining.

THE SCHOOL AS A WORKPLACE

Frequently, evening news programs run stories about decrepit school buildings where teachers work in the worst of conditions. We know that administrators do want the newest, cleanest, and most welcoming facilities for their teachers and students. Sometimes that is not possible. However, the goal of having good facilities is critically important. Consider the difference in the following scenarios:

1. In a Midwestern town, where the school year begins in early August, there is no air conditioning in teachers' classrooms. There is air conditioning in the principal's office and in the superintendent's office building. When asked in a meeting why air conditioning was not on the list for building updates, the superintendent said it wasn't needed. The teacher then asked, "Why is needed in administrative offices then?" "Well, we couldn't work without it," was the response. This is what lowers teacher morale!
2. When teachers write their end-of-year evaluation of the school, many complain about the condition of the teachers' lounge and workroom. A teacher simply asks if she and her friends can paint the rooms themselves over the summer and bring in some donated furniture. The principal is delighted by the suggestion and offers to help move furniture and buy lunch for all who paint. This raises teacher morale.

Administrators have tough jobs and their jobs have become increasingly difficult. Most administrators deserve a gold star for their work, and they often deserve more consideration and respect from their employees than they receive. Creating a workplace that is collegial and positive in all respects will also help to provide support for the administrators from their teachers. There are many teachers who praise their principals frequently, hoping that they don't leave the school for another job. Retaining effective principals helps to retain good teachers.

SUMMARY POINTS FOR SUCCESS

1. Today's teachers want, and will demand, a clean and positive workplace.
2. Teachers want their voices heard. Ask for input on decisions where the teacher does have significant frontline experience.
3. When teachers are asked for input, report their recommendations back and discuss possible changes.

4. Beginning teachers report that supportive colleagues are a reason that they stay in their school and the teaching profession. Create opportunities for collegiality and teacher-to-teacher support.

5. Communication is always a key to improving the workplace. Plan for positive feedback to teachers on a frequent basis. Don't let a teacher with a negative, toxic personality become a ringleader or teachers' lounge queen.

Chapter Ten

Teacher Longevity

> In other words, the *more* supported English teachers felt, the *less* likely they
> were to be considered a high risk for attrition than those receiving *less* support.
> —Hancock and Scherff (2010, p. 328)

Stories abound about teachers who taught for thirty or forty years in the same school, and sometimes even in the same classroom. These teachers often taught generations within a family and their legacies enhanced the school's reputation. As opposed to the "revolving door" of today's teachers in some districts, these career teachers must have found jobs that fit their needs and those of the school. What contributes to teacher longevity and how is resilience a factor to retaining effective teachers?

Rinke's (2014) work raises "the question of whether the teaching profession is once again returning to its historical roots as a temporary occupation" (p. 1). She purports that beginning educators may enter teaching "with the idea of temporarily exploring teaching" (p. 1). Since women and minorities have more opportunities in other professional sectors than ever before, teaching may be viewed as just a short-term first job for some who would have made a long-term career of teaching in the past.

The trend of having multiple jobs and holding a job for just a chapter of one's life appeals to today's Millennials. They may seek to teach to make a difference in the world, but only for a few years before pursuing something else.

Programs like Teach for America have provided a prestigious venue for short-term teaching followed by an exit with teaching as a line on one's resume as proof of "giving back." If teachers themselves have short-term goals for their teaching careers, it may be doubly difficult to retain the best and the brightest in the profession.

While no one can predict the complete course of their lives or of their careers, Rinke's (2014) work indicates that teachers' plans matter. She suggests that both teacher educators and employers focus on getting candidates and new hires to envision their professional career pathways. This might imply that employers look at how teachers earned their certification, and that students who have always wanted to be teachers and who majored in education as undergraduates may have long-term teaching goals in mind. New teachers' career plans will definitely be shaped by their induction into the profession and the quality of the workplace they encounter.

Some research has examined how teachers move along career paths from novices to experts who stay in the classroom. Steffy, Wolfe, Pasch, and Enz (2000) created a model with the following stages of teacher development: novice, apprentice, professional, expert, distinguished, and emeritus. For each level, unique professional development supported the retention of the teachers in that stage. Growth opportunities for the teacher, followed by reflection and renewal, were integral to sustaining teachers in each level of their career.

In other words, a one-size-fits-all workshop is not what teachers need. The ideas provided throughout this book for extended mentoring, mentoring in teams, professional learning communities, collegial observations, book studies, and teacher leadership opportunities can provide the development for teachers at each stage of their careers.

STRESS AND RESILIENCE

While the Peace Corps coined the phrase, "the toughest job you'll ever love," it may be completely apropos to the entire teaching profession. Teaching is a tough, demanding job, even under the best of circumstances. The accountability placed on teachers to raise student achievement while working with an increasingly diverse student population creates tremendous stress. The severity and the complexity of teachers' stress and anxiety have increased dramatically. Teachers need training in stress management for themselves and training in how to help their students cope with stress.

Consider weaving stress management into the professional development sessions already offered in the school. Stress management is a must for the ongoing new teacher workshops. Mentoring a new teacher can be stressful, so sessions on stress management need to be built into the support seminars for the veteran teachers who are supporting new hires. A book study or professional learning community can read and research the topic—hopefully with some hands-on activities and practical ideas for those in the group.

What might a short workshop on stress management look like and who can teach it? Every school district has counselors and many may be trained in this sort of work. Look inside the district before hiring expensive one-shot consultants. Consider the following for helping teachers with stress management:

1. Voluntary attendance at a workshop may be critical in getting buy-in about stress management.
2. Confidentiality is a big issue when working with individuals to minimize stress to improve performance. The leader of any offerings must be aware of confidentiality issues.
3. Helping teachers to identify specific stressors and what to do about them is a good starting point in stress management. (See appendix 10.1.)
4. Time management is tied directly to stress management. Provide seminars or discussion groups on this topic. (See appendix 10.2 for a sample activity.)
5. Allow and encourage open discussion about stressful issues.
6. Accept teachers' feelings of helplessness, hopelessness, and depression. Then, provide support and help.
7. Consider some basic stress relievers: healthy choices available for lunch, a private lunchroom for teachers, healthy snacks at meetings, access to a gym or pool, flexibility for a teacher to take a short walk over lunch or during preparation time, availability of counselors for one-on-one conversations.
8. Encourage membership in professional organizations and support attendance at conferences and workshops away from the district.
9. Pay people for extra duties and summer work. Extra bonuses are rare in teaching, but are very well received.
10. Praise employees for work well done and say thank you often. Provide inspirational articles and books to teachers.

All too often, teachers feel completely overwhelmed and beleaguered by their jobs. They begin to feel hopeless with regard to being respected for their work and getting students to achieve. Teachers want and need to feel successful. By identifying and isolating the factors causing stress, positive interventions can be designed to help teachers survive and succeed at their jobs in spite of the stressors. Many times a teacher will quit a job even though they still proclaim to love teaching. It may be that work factors or stress issues seem or are insurmountable to them.

Very few school administrators have received training in how to support teachers with regard to stress management. Many principals reading this chapter may say, "This is NOT my job. I hire adults and they should be able to take care of themselves." Times have changed and creating opportunities to help and support teachers with the stress of their jobs has now become another part of the administrator's job. This adds to the already overloaded list of duties for the school administrators and creates stress for them.

What about resilience? A resilient teacher faces challenges and difficulties and continues to be effective on the job. More has probably been written about resilient students than resiliency in teachers. Writing about student resiliency, Truebridge (2016) notes that there are protective factors that "contribute to the healthy and successful development and emergence of the individual's personal competencies and strengths" that will contribute to overall resiliency (p. 23). These factors fit well for enhancing teacher resiliency:

1. having social competence (empathy, forgiveness)
2. problem-solving abilities (critical thinking)
3. autonomy (self-awareness; self-efficacy)
4. sense of purpose and future (goal direction, optimism)

Truebridge (2016) defines resiliency as a process:

> The internal process consists of tapping into one's personal strengths, attributes, and past experiences. The external process involves making available and tapping into school, family, community opportunities, resources, supports, and services. The process of integrating resilience requires a shift in attitudes about the current approach being used in a school. (p. 23)

To further explain this in regard to teachers, a resilient teacher is one who has strong personal strengths, or what may simply be called "inner strength." A resilient teacher has the experience and background to overcome challenges and charge forward in a tough teaching situation.

What few schools have provided in the past are the external factors for building resilient teachers. The availability of supports, as listed by Truebridge, might take the shape of professional development in the school or counseling for teachers. Community support might mean reduced-price gym memberships, free library cards, more teacher appreciation events, and recognition of teachers by civic organizations.

Most importantly, the idea that school administrators need to have resiliency supports in their long-term retention plans is imperative. While one hopes that all adults build their own frameworks to remain positive and resilient, many teachers are going to need the framework provided by the employer.

As employers look at who is entering the teaching force, they need to understand who is going to college, and the issues of today's college students. The severity and complexity of stress and anxiety in today's college students is overwhelming. Large numbers of college students enter college with diagnosed anxiety issues, needing therapeutic interventions throughout higher education.

College professors routinely refer students to counseling centers when the students simply "melt down" during finals week or other stressful times. The students who pop a Xanax before a tough class or who can't sleep without pills is alarming. These issues do not disappear when a student graduates and becomes a new employee. New teachers face tremendous stress, and offering supports to build their resiliency may become standard operating procedures in schools dedicated to retaining teachers.

SHOULD ALL TEACHERS BE RETAINED?

A 2016 *Washington Post* article title proclaimed, "Sometimes, teacher turnover is a good thing" (Brown, 2016). The article discussed a study indicating that weak teachers need to leave their classrooms and the profession.

> The departure of teachers who score poorly on IMPACT [a teacher evaluation system] is actually a good thing because student scores on math and reading tests tend to improve substantially after such teachers depart . . . .
>
> In contrast, student scores tend to drop slightly when high-performing teachers leave their assignments for another school or district, presumably because it is difficult to find replacements who are as effective. (paragraphs 2 and 3)

While this is just one study, it does point to the value of retaining the highly effective teacher.

The retention of teachers with negative attitudes affects teacher morale, especially if those teachers work closely with new hires. Of course, not every single aspect of personnel selection and retention can be controlled. Schools are big entities, often with huge faculties serving thousands of students. In large schools and school systems, the role of teacher leaders may be especially important. A department chair can work closely with a grade level, or within a discipline, to create a positive, healthy climate and support for a smaller group of teachers. Many teachers survive, and thrive, because of the colleagues and support found on their hallway or in their discipline.

The research on teacher retention, teacher burnout, teacher dropout, and teachers' jobs is abundant. The gap seems to be in how to implement what is known in the hectic, stressful environments of today's schools. There is a need for some paradigm shifts. The hiring process must become a longer, more involved process based on candidates' past experience and expertise. Retention does begin with hiring the right people for positions.

Induction is most effective when it is an extended process and when veteran teachers are trained and supported to mentor teachers. The development of teacher leaders will provide the incentive for many to stay in teaching, especially today's Millennials who want to have input and want to affect immediate change.

Building collegial workplaces where teachers observe and support each other is a retention strategy. Supportive administrators who observe and implement fair evaluation practices are critically important to their faculty members.

Teachers and administrators deal with all students who walk through the school's doors, and today's students bring tremendous issues with them. Students who come from homes where they are unwanted, uncared for, and unloved, need tremendous amounts of nurturing in school just to survive, much less to begin learning. Faced with these challenges, it is hard to retain effective teachers in schools. But again, models exist for supporting teachers who can not only do the job of teaching, but do it with remarkable success.

Concluding Essay

When a principal said that teachers who don't get jobs don't deserve them, it prompted me to write an essay about teachers' qualifications. A discussion of what new hires deserve from the school as a workplace completes the essay. The essay follows:

My student teachers continually worry about getting their first teaching jobs. While dutifully creating their résumés, cover letters, and interview portfolios throughout the senior year in college, they begin to network with administrators. One student teacher recently remarked, "A principal told me that I shouldn't worry so much about getting a job. He said that the teachers who are not getting jobs don't deserve them." This statement prompted me to think about teacher candidates and their qualifications to work in schools.

Certificated/licensed teachers deserve jobs. While tremendous debate remains about the true qualifications of fully licensed teachers, having a system of teacher certification in each state probably remains the best first test of whether or not a teacher is ready to assume all of the duties of a classroom teacher.

Would you even consider seeing a physician who wasn't licensed or having your legal work done by an attorney who hadn't passed the bar? Why tout the value of a "bright, energetic, well-meaning" candidate who didn't bother to study education long enough to get certified to teach?

Well-educated candidates deserve jobs. What, of course, is the definition of "well-educated"? Certainly having at least a bachelor's degree level of knowledge of the subject matter to be taught is a requisite to teach that subject. Candidates should also have sound general education skills. They should know how to write and speak well. They should have a strong enough background in the humanities and the sciences that they can relate the subject to the big world around them. The general education background should give them an appreciation for all subjects, and for learning.

Candidates who know pedagogy deserve jobs. Just knowing calculus does not necessarily mean that one can teach it. The academic language of teaching changes rapidly, and a strong candidate is current with national, state, and local curriculum standards, as well as teaching methods.

There is a reason that employers ask candidates to describe their classroom management plans and to tell about the routines and procedures that they have used successfully in a school. A candidate without classroom management strategies may not get to teach the steps in the well-written lesson plan. Management, planning, assessment, and differentiation are necessary pedagogical skills needed by teachers.

Candidates with a strong work ethic deserve jobs. Teaching is not easy, nor does the day end with a 3 p.m. dismissal bell. Teaching is hard work, and it is certainly not always fun. Students who know their teacher is "there for them" tend to gain more from all aspects of school.

Teachers who are professionals deserve to be hired. Teachers should be well-dressed individuals who arrive on time and are organized for busy days. Professional teachers continue to take classes, earn advanced degrees, and become involved in school governance. Rather than just complaining publicly about the schools, they work to improve their situations.

Caring teachers deserve jobs. The word "care" has many definitions. Teachers of young children are certainly caregivers, and high school teachers deal with a "tough love" kind of caring. Teachers must model "caring" and instill a sense of caring into students of all ages.

After my student shared the quote from her conversation with the principal, I wished that I had the chance to ask him a question. I would have asked, "What kinds of schools deserve the well-educated, caring, highly qualified teachers that accredited institutions are producing?" The answer to that question might have included the following topics.

New hires deserve a supportive induction program. Professional development for new teachers should be developed according to their needs, and should be ongoing throughout the first five years—not just a one-shot orientation program.

New hires deserve a qualified, trained mentor to help them learn their way in the new school. Both the new teacher and the mentor need release time to work together, because learning to teach is a process. The learning curve the first two years is very steep.

It almost goes without saying that new teachers need good salaries, clean workplaces, and secretarial support. The quality of the workplace is an issue for all employees, and teachers deserve to be treated as professionals.

Teachers deserve the respect and support of the communities where they work. Positive parental involvement is critical in the education of a student.

Teachers deserve a fair and valid evaluation system. While teachers are accountable for student learning, there are a myriad of other factors that contribute to student success that are outside of the teacher's control.

Teachers deserve credit for the tremendous work that they do every day. They succeed against all odds on most days.

Perhaps when schools become more collegial, professional workplaces, more candidates will want to start, and continue, their careers there. A colleague of mine has often said, "Schools get the teachers they deserve." It is food for thought. We do know two things for certain—students deserve effective teachers and effective teachers need to be retained in schools.

SUMMARY POINTS FOR SUCCESS

1. While some teachers do work for thirty to forty years in the profession, today's new teachers may not have long-term career plans.
2. Schools need to build stress management supports into their professional development offerings and into the school culture.
3. The creation of resiliency in teachers is two-fold. Teachers need to build their own inner resiliency through their beliefs, and schools need to plan ways to help teachers with resiliency support systems.
4. Not all teachers should be retained, but the retention of effective teachers is critically important.
5. The research on teacher retention is plentiful. Researchers know what keeps teachers in classrooms and why teachers leave. The research has to be used to formulate plans for teacher retention.

Appendix 3.1—Preliminary Interview Checklist

List 3 to 5 bullet points that are positive attributes of your schools system.

1.
2.
3.
4.
5.

How can these points be added to questions asked in the preliminary interview?

Basic preliminary interview questions may include:

1. Tell us about your experience with this grade level or subject area.
2. Describe your approach to planning a lesson and then to long-term planning.
3. Tell about the best classroom management you have seen or used. What made that classroom a friendly, yet businesslike, environment where students were engaged?
4. How have you encouraged students to learn difficult material?
5. What experience have you had preparing students for standardized tests?
6. Describe your work with _____. (Name a special population here—low-income, special education, gifted, etc.)
7. What interested you about a position in our school/district?

For any interview, the same questions must be asked of all candidates, in the same order. Add an evaluation component, such as Weak Answer, Average Answer, or Target Answer, or a numeric scale to the final template.

Appendix 3.2—Question Bank for Early Elementary School Positions

1. Tell about your teaching experience with preschool through second grade.
2. Describe the developmental stages of young children.
3. Describe a lesson that you have taught that was developmentally appropriate for this young age group. Why did the lesson succeed?
4. What types of routines and procedures have you implemented in a classroom?
5. What types of rules and consequences have you implemented in a classroom?
6. What have you taken from your own experiences in early elementary school and implemented in a classroom? Why?
7. Our teachers are very enthusiastic about teaching with _____. What is your experience with this program?
8. At our school, grade level planning is important. What are your experiences working with others in planning?
9. Describe a recent success you have had with an individual student who was having difficulty with something.
10. How have you communicated with parents? What special issues arise when communicating with parents of young children?
11. Tell about your experiences of being supervised and evaluated. What have you learned from past evaluations?
12. Our teachers say that the best part of teaching here is _____. How do you respond to their comment?

Appendix 3.3—Question Bank for Upper Elementary School Positions

1. Describe your approach(es) to teaching reading.
2. Tell us about a lesson plan where reading/language arts was taught. What was the primary objective of that lesson and how did you know that students achieved the objective?
3. How have you taught math? Describe a math lesson that was successful.
4. What are some motivational strategies that have worked well for you with upper elementary students? In other words, what have you done in the past to engage students this age in their learning?
5. How have you prepared students for standardized testing?
6. What were the standardized test results in classrooms where you have worked? What have you learned from reviewing those test results?
7. What routines and procedures have you implemented in a classroom? Why?
8. What rules and consequences have you implemented in a classroom? Were they successful?
9. How have you integrated science and social studies into lessons?
10. Describe a success story that you have had with a student in an upper elementary grade (any topic—reading, math, behavior, attendance, etc.).
11. How have you communicated with parents about their child's progress?
12. Our upper elementary teachers have achieved good results with _____. Please share your experiences with _____.

Appendix 3.4—Question Bank for Middle School Positions

1. Describe a lesson you have taught in a middle school classroom. Why did it go well? What would change if you were to teach it again?
2. Our teachers work in grade-level teams. What has been your experience working and planning on a team?
3. Middle school students are at an awkward age. Describe their developmental level and how you have worked with students at this level with regard to their maturity.
4. Tell about a lesson or activity that motivated your students to learn. Why did it motivate them?
5. How have you assessed student learning? How have you prepared students for standardized testing?
6. How have you differentiated instruction for students in this age group?
7. What has been your experience working with special education co-teachers?
8. Describe past evaluations that you have had. What did you learn or change from an observation by a supervisor?
9. What has motivated you to work with middle school students?
10. How have you communicated successfully with parents/families of your students?
11. Describe one of the most important things you learned from your student teaching experience.
12. Our middle school teachers are very excited about _____. What is your experience with _____?

Appendix 3.5—Question Bank for High School Positions

1. Describe a successful lesson you have taught in your discipline. Why was it successful?
2. What are some significant standards or topics in your field that must be taught well and how have you included those standards/topics in your long-term planning?
3. Describe the positive ways that you have organized and managed a classroom.
4. What rules, consequences, and positive reinforcements have you used in a classroom?
5. How have you motivated students to stay in school and graduate?
6. How have you successfully communicated with parents/families of your students?
7. Tell about your experience preparing high school students for standardized, graduation, or end-of-course tests.
8. Describe your past evaluations and what you learned after an observation or evaluation by a supervisor.
9. How have you differentiated lessons to meet the needs of all students?
10. Tell about a success you have experienced with a student (academic or behavioral).
11. How do you incorporate technology into your classes?
12. Describe an example of informal and formal assessments that you have used with your students.

Appendix 3.6—Question Bank for Special Areas

Art, Music, Health, and Physical Education

1. Describe a classroom/gym/field where you have taught in terms of the organization needed for your field of study.
2. Tell about planning the curriculum for your area based on the standards in your field.
3. Many say that it is hard to give a letter grade for _____. How have you assessed and graded your students?
4. How have you motivated students to participate in your area and achieve success?
5. Walk me through a typical 50-minute class in your field. Please include common routines and procedures that you have used.
6. What experience have you had communicating with parents/families about their children's success, or lack of success, in your classes?
7. How do you defend the need for your area to be included in a school's curriculum?
8. Our teachers of _____ work closely with the teachers of academic subjects to align as many topics as possible with the topics in other classes. Describe your experience working with other teachers.
9. How have you created adaptations for special needs students in your classes?
10. How have you showcased your students' work for the school or community?

11. Address any special safety concerns for working with students in art/ music/HPE (traveling with band, sports injuries, etc.)

Appendix 3.7—Question Bank for Special Education Interviews

The vocabulary for special education positions varies widely. Questions need specificity to each job opening. General examples include:

1. Describe your experience as a special education teacher working with another teacher in his/her classroom.
2. Tell about your experience with procedures for diagnosing students with special needs.
3. Describe your experience creating individual educational plans (IEPs) for students.
4. Explain a specific success you have had with a student and how you achieved that success.
5. Discuss your experiences with improving student behavior for a specific student.
6. Tell about your work with students with a diagnosis of _____ (ADD/ADHD, autism, etc.).
7. Describe a fairly common adaptation you have used for a student or students in a regular education classroom.
8. How have you differentiated instruction or assessment for a student or students?
9. Describe your experience with a successful parent conference about a student. What made the conference successful?
10. Describe a past evaluation that you have had. What did you learn or improve because of that observation or evaluation?

Appendix 3.8 — Evaluation of Candidate Answers

To build an evaluation form for preliminary or on-site interview questions, consider the following models:

For each interview question, rate the candidate's answer on a scale of 1 to 5, where 1 indicates no experience or expertise with the question's content, and 5 indicates outstanding experience and past expertise.
No experience/expertise 1——2——3——4——5 Outstanding experience/expertise
Write out each question, with a blank for the rating of the answer.
1. Tell about the best lesson you have taught and why it went well. _____

The same format may be completed for a scale of 1 to 7. Adding breadth to the evaluation system can create a more accurate picture of the candidate's experience and expertise.

Creation of a three-category system also works well.
For each question, rate the candidate's answers as unacceptable, acceptable, or on target/outstanding.
1. Tell about the best lesson you have taught and why it went well.
_____ unacceptable _____ acceptable _____ outstanding
With this system, totals then indicate how many answers were in each category.

Appendix 3.9—Creating a Rubric to Evaluate Answers

The use of rubrics to evaluate candidates' answers to interview questions can add to the validity of the evaluation, as the interviewer has determined in advance the necessary experience and expertise necessary for the question topic. For example,

- Question: How have you differentiated the instructional content, process, product, or learning environment to meet individual needs?

Exemplary Answer: (5 points)
The candidate provides clear, concrete examples of differentiation from past teaching. The candidate's answers evidence providing students with opportunities to engage in critical thinking and creative activities, all of which are tailored to individual needs. The candidate may have shared his/her work with other teachers. The candidate expresses consistency in providing examples, such as "I build differentiation into *every* plan."

Proficient/Acceptable Answer: (3 points)
The candidate can provide examples of challenging and supporting individual student's learning. There is consistency to the candidate's examples of appropriate differentiation of content and skills that address individual differences.

Developing/Needs Improvement (1 point)
The candidate has limited examples of providing content or developing individual learning differences in his/her past teaching. The teacher shows inconsistency in differentiation of instruction or assessment.

Unacceptable (0 points)

The candidate does not use the vocabulary of differentiation and does not provide examples of challenging, remediating, or enhancing individual student learning. The candidate expresses the idea of "teaching to the middle of a class," not individualizing instruction.

Appendix 3.10—Sample Survey of New Hires

Please rate your hiring experience on a scale of 1 to 5, with 1 indicating complete disagreement and 5 indicating complete agreement.

1. The communication from the district was efficient and helpful throughout the hiring process. _____

2. The job advertisement was clear and accurate. _____

3. I was treated respectfully by all who interviewed me. _____

4. Based on my hiring experience, I would recommend this district to friends seeking teaching jobs. _____

5. The district website provided me with accurate and clear information. _____

6. After hiring, the district provided me with clear directions for completion of mandatory paperwork. _____

7. The timeline from the submission of my application to being hired was a reasonable one. _____

8. Overall, my experience of being hired was very positive. _____

What suggestions do you have to improve the hiring process of our district?

What other comments do you have regarding the advertisement of our teaching jobs, our preliminary interviews, and final on-site interviews?

Appendix 3.11—Review of Annual Hiring

(To be completed by all involved in the hiring process.)

Please rate your experience with hiring new teachers on a scale of 1 to 5, with 1 indicating complete disagreement and 5 indicating complete agreement.

1. I felt prepared and trained for my role in hiring new teachers. _____

2. The district provided me with sample questions and interview protocols. _____

3. Ample time was provided to assess each candidate's strengths in interviews. _____

4. My input was valued and used in the final decision-making process. _____

5. Our hiring process is well organized. _____

6. Our website, or other online presence, is a strong recruitment tool. _____

7. This year's hiring timeline was efficient and effective. _____

8. This year's new hires should be effective, based on our hiring practice. _____

What changes do you recommend for next year's hiring season?

Please consider our district's hiring practice to your own hiring experience. What are we doing well?

Please add any other relevant comments.

Appendix 4.1—Evaluation of New Teacher Orientation

On a scale of 1 to 5, where 1 indicates complete disagreement and 5 indicates complete agreement, please rate the following statements:

1. The help I received over the summer regarding moving to the district was important and helpful. _____

2. The help I received about paperwork, insurance, payroll, and background checks was helpful. _____

3. Overall, the orientation sessions before the first day of school were very helpful. _____

4. The session about _____ was very helpful. _____

5. I appreciated the time provided me to work in my classroom. _____

6. The time spent with my mentor teacher in orientation was helpful. _____

Now, please provide some comments on the following:

1. The most helpful part of orientation was _____ because . . .

2. For me, the least helpful part of orientation was _____ because . . .

3. For next year's orientation, I recommend . . .

What else would you like the orientation organizers and teachers to know about orientation?

Appendix 4.2 — New Teacher Orientation Active Learning Strategies

1. Have participants introduce themselves as they will to their students on the first day of class. Stress the importance of those first moments of class.
2. Have participants develop an outline of their script for the first part of the first day of school. They must include how they will introduce themselves and how they will get students to learn each other's names.
3. Have teachers make their classroom management posters. These posters should include rules, positive supports, and consequences in line with the school/district guidelines.
4. Role-play what to do if a student misbehaves on the first day of class. Examples include: a student who runs into the room and throws books down; a student who refuses to follow the first directions given; a student who will not sit down; a student who uses inappropriate language.
5. Have some "what to do when" scenarios. These include: what to do when you are sick; what to do when a student refuses to leave the room; how best to talk to parents; what to do in a fire drill or other emergency.
6. Briefly discuss the teacher evaluation system. Explain when teachers will get training on the evaluation instrument and what to expect in an evaluative observation.
7. Role-play the types of things you can ask your mentor and what he/she can do for you.
8. Role-play some violence prevention strategies and emergency procedures.

Appendix 5.1—Mentor Application

Do you remember your first year of teaching? Or years two through five? Our district is building a pool of trained mentors to support new teachers through their first five years of teaching. Please answer the following questions for consideration as a mentor in the future. (Add information about due dates, length of service, released time, and payment for work.)

1. Why do you want to be a mentor teacher?
2. What is an activity you would like to complete with a new hire before the school year begins? (Be specific about working in a classroom, etc.)
3. How would you encourage a new hire with regard to _____ (curriculum, testing, student diversity, time management, etc.)?
4. What do you consider a strength of your teaching career that you would like to share with new hires?
5. Our mentors are encouraged to teach one of the new teacher seminars. Please list one or two topics you feel comfortable teaching to the group of new hires.
6. Please list experience you have had working with a student teacher, a practicum student, or a new hire.
7. Please list your professional memberships and any conferences or professional meetings that you have attended recently. Did you present at any of these?

Appendix 5.2—Evaluation of Mentor Training

On a scale of 1 to 5, where 1 indicates disagreement and 5 represents complete agreement, please rate the following:

1. The mentor training prepared me well for my role as a mentor. _____

2. The length of the training was about right. _____

3. Hearing from recent new hires was a valuable part of the training. _____

4. Hearing from other veteran teachers or mentors was valuable. _____

5. I learned new material about teaching/district issues in mentor training. _____

6. The mentor training was well organized and a good use of time. _____

7. My experience was appreciated and valued during mentor training. _____

8. I would be interested in participating as a trainer of mentors in the future. _____

9. The meals and snacks were good. _____

10. The location/venue for mentor training was comfortable. _____

1. What was the most useful part of the mentor training for you? Why?

2. Were any parts of the mentor training unnecessary for you? Why?

3. What else would you like to share about the mentor training?

Appendix 5.3—Mentor and New Teacher Discussion List

1. What needs to be ready for the first day of school?
2. What is the script for the first day of school? What will the teacher say and do?
3. Make a classroom management plan together. It includes rules, consequences, and positive supports for student behavior. Make a poster of the plan for the room.
4. Share sample parent letters and read the new teacher's letter to parents.
5. What procedures and routines are needed in this grade/subject? How do students get from class to class here or how does the teacher plan smooth transitions?
6. Where are the books and teaching materials? Where does the teacher get more supplies?
7. How does the technology work in this room/building?
8. What are the school policies on major discipline issues?
9. Who are the teacher's contacts for special education, ESOL, or other?
10. What does the teacher do when he/she wakes up sick? What are the guidelines and who do they call?
11. Talk about testing—weekly, by semester, and standardized tests.
12. When will the teacher and mentor observe each other?
13. What will the teacher's formal observations by the principal or department chair be like?
14. What materials should the teacher keep for student records?
15. What are parent conferences like here? When and how are they scheduled?
16. How should the teacher communicate with the principal?

17. If a crisis happens, what are the basic steps to take?
18. Talk about how grades are determined and distributed here—especially online grades.

Appendix 5.4—Evaluation of the Mentoring Program

(Mentor's Perspective)

On a scale of 1 to 5, where 1 indicates disagreement and 5 represents complete agreement, please rate the following:

1. I felt well prepared for mentoring from the district training.   _____

2. My new teacher understood what I could and could not do for   _____
support.

3. My new teacher and I met or talked at least once a week.   _____

4. The work my new teacher and I did before school started was   _____
important.

5. I was adequately paid for my mentoring duties (with time or   _____
money).

6. I would like to work as a mentor with another new teacher.   _____

7. I observed my new teacher at least three times this year.   _____

8. My new teacher observed me at least three times this year.   _____

What are the strengths of our district's mentoring program?

What would you like to see added or changed to improve the program?

Would you like to have a larger role in the mentoring program (teaching more seminars, training new mentors, working with young mentors, etc.)?

Any other recommendations for the mentoring program?

Appendix 5.5—Evaluation of the Mentoring Program

(New Teacher's Perspective)

On a scale of 1 to 5, where 1 indicates disagreement and 5 represents complete agreement, please rate the following:

1. I understood what to expect from the mentoring program. _____

2. I knew what my mentor could and could not do for me. _____

3. My mentor and I met or talked at least once a week. _____

4. The work my mentor and I did before school started was important. _____

5. I had adequate time to work with my mentor. _____

6. I would like to work with my mentor another year. _____

7. I observed my mentor at least three times this year. _____

8. My mentor observed me at least three times this year. _____

What would you like to see added or changed to improve the program?

Would you like to be a junior mentor to a new hire in the next year or two?

Any other recommendations for the mentoring program?

Appendix 6.1—New Teacher Professional Development Survey

On a scale of 1 to 5, where 1 indicates disagreement and 5 represents complete agreement, please rate the following. (We will develop workshops on those topics with the lowest average scores.)

1. Setting up my classroom and establishing routines and procedures that work are strengths of mine.   _____

2. I have had much experience in creating and using a classroom management plan.   _____

3. I am very comfortable creating lesson plans that work well.   _____

4. I am very comfortable with using a variety of teaching methods.   _____

5. I know and have used multiple strategies for motivating students with low achievement.   _____

6. I know and have used multiple strategies for working with special education/inclusion students.   _____

7. I feel very comfortable with strategies for teaching English language learners.   _____

List other topics specific to the district.
I would really like to see the following topics included in this year's workshops. (Circle yes or no.)

1. More about discipline and behavior management.   Yes   No

2. Expectations for improving test scores.   Yes   No

3. The district evaluation guidelines for reemployment /   Yes   No
tenure.

4. Student engagement strategies.   Yes   No

5. Improving reading comprehension practices.   Yes   No

Appendix 6.2 — Lesson Plan on Parent Communication and Conferences

(2–3 hours)

As teachers enter the room, they see a list called "Today we will" on the board or screen. The list is:

Introductions and focus activity
The many ways to communicate with parents
The parent conferences in our school
Role-plays of parent calls and conferences
Conclusions and takeaway ideas

Focus activity: (posted on screen or board)
As you enter, please write out the best opportunity you have had to communicate something positive with a parent or guardian. Then, write out a challenge you are concerned about or a question you have about communications with parents.

I. Introductions and focus

- Begin by having each person share the focus activity answers with one other person. Then, those two people share with another pair of teachers. After time for sharing, have each group of four tell one best opportunity and one question/concern.

II. Instructor presents how we share information and communicate with parents.

- What do we call parents today? With many children not living with their own parents, we must be careful with the word "parent." Caregiver? Guardian? Discuss the district's demographics and what the district perceives as best practice in addressing families with communication.
- Discuss traditional newsletters and syllabi sent home. Are they mailed or sent electronically? Show examples from current teachers.
- Discuss social media communication and concerns.
- Discuss the district's website and school websites and how teachers can post on those sites.
- Provide a template for making parent phone calls. This template should be completed before making a call and should be kept as documentation in the student's file.

III. Parent conferences

- Provide teachers with a template for conducting parent conferences. The template might include: time, date, location, something positive about the student, stated reason for the conference, what the teacher has already done with the student about the issue, what the teacher recommends as next steps for the student's issue, parent input about the student, parent support for next steps, conclusion of conference. Provide a handout of the template and an electronic copy. Provide information about who, if anyone, needs a copy of the completed form after the conference. Stress the need for valid documentation of conferences.

IV. Role-play parent phone calls and conferences. Examples:

- A parent calls the teacher and states, "My daughter says that she is probably not going to get an A in your class. This will be her first grade below an A. Can you give her extra credit so that she does get an A this grading period?" Your response on the phone?
- As a teacher, you call a parent to discuss the student's very low attendance in class. The student has missed six days in one month, with no actual reason. The parent is difficult. Act out the parent's and the teacher's roles.

V. Conclusion
For the conclusion, the instructor reads each of the following scenarios. Teachers work in pairs or small groups to vote on each scenario. The questions are: Would you contact the parent to discuss this issue? If so, how would you contact the parent—letter, call, e-mail, or conference?

- A 1st grade student never has a pencil or any required supplies.
- A 3rd grade student refused to take a spelling test.

- A 9th grade student wrote "Teacher, you are a b——" on his/her paper.
- An 8th grade student scored the winning touchdown at a home football game.
- Your student got his/her first A on an assignment after weeks of lower grades.
- You are told that the student will be out for ten days with a major illness.

Add other scenarios that may be unique to the district, such as communicating with parents who do not speak English, military families, and so forth.

Appendix 6.3—Lesson Plan for New Teacher Workshop on Classroom Management

(2–3 hours)

As teachers enter the room, they see a list called "Today we will" on the board or screen. The list is:

Introductions and focus activity
Harry Wong and routines and procedures
The classroom management plan
Special issues with our students
Role-plays of challenges
What is your takeaway from today?

Focus activity: (posted on screen or board)

- Write out the best classroom management strategy that you are using every day.
- Write out a challenge you still have with a student or class with regard to management.

I. Introductions and focus

- For small groups, each person can introduce themselves by name and grade/subject. Also, what do you do to focus YOUR class?

- Explain that today's workshop had a routine that can be used every day to improve management. That routine is posting four to six things that will be done and having a focus activity to start the class.
- Now, write a focus activity that you can use tomorrow in your class.

II. Discuss the need for Harry Wong's style of classroom management routines and procedures.

- Show a video clip of Wong, if available.
- Have teachers pair up, or work in groups of three, to discuss their best procedures and routines.
- Ask where the problems are and where they still need to make a workable routine.

III. The classroom management plan. Each classroom needs a posted classroom management plan. This plan should have three to five rules, consequences for when rules are broken, and positive reinforcements for when students work well.

- Have a veteran teacher show her plan and explain how it is used.
- Have teachers make posters for their rooms, if they didn't do this at an orientation session.
- Show examples of plans from Lee Canter's *Assertive Discipline* (2009) or other book.
- Sample rules:

    1. Keep hands, feet, and objects to yourself.
    2. Use a reasonable speaking voice in the room.
    3. Be in your assigned seat/place for each activity.

- Sample consequences:

    1. Warning from the teacher.
    2. Loss of regular seat.
    3. Must have silent lunch.
    4. School-monitored detention.
    5. Parent call/principal visit.

- Sample positive reinforcements:

    1. Free reading time.
    2. Positive note home.
    3. Build your positives and earn free school supplies.

IV. Classroom management issues with our students

- For this part of the workshop, have someone speak to the issues common to your school.
- Then, have teachers write out scenes that they have seen in their classrooms that address these common issues.
- Solve the scenes or discuss them.

V. Role-play scenes

- Role-play scenes from above, or have the workshop instructor bring in sample scenes to role-play. The importance is having the teachers use the exact words that they would use when speaking with students involved in an issue.
- Example: A student says, "What are you picking on me for? Sam did the same thing." What do you say to the student?

VI. Conclusion and takeaways

- Good conclusions are made by the teachers themselves. Have teachers do this in groups of three and read what they learned, or have teachers walk around the room writing their learning on posters.

Keys for success for any new teacher workshop include having the teachers completely engaged with the learning and each other. This also models how they should be teaching.

Appendix 6.4—Year One Induction Workshop Evaluation

On a scale of 1 to 5, where 1 indicates disagreement and 5 represents complete agreement, please rate the following:

1. I found the workshops to be very beneficial. ____

2. The length of the workshops was appropriate. ____

3. The timing of the workshops was appropriate (once a month). ____

4. The topics were very helpful to me. ____

5. The workshop coordinator was organized and made good use of ____
time.

6. The guest speakers provided very useful information. ____

7. Our group developed supportive ties with one another. ____

8. Even if not required, I would have attended these workshops. ____

Now, answer with short responses.

1. The most beneficial workshop was the one about _____
   because . . .

2. The least beneficial workshop was the one about _____
   because . . .

3. To improve next year's workshops, I would recommend . . .

4. More time needs to be devoted to _____ in the induction workshops.

5. Do you have any other comments or suggestions for this program?

Appendix 7.1—Observation Preconference Worksheet

Date and time of observation:
Grade/subject level: _____ number of students: _____
Standard(s) addressed in lesson:
Teacher goal:
Student learning objective:

1. What is the observer to watch for in this lesson? (List specifics, such as observing for number of questions asked; number of times class is interrupted for behavior issues; informal assessment of student learning; other.)

2. How will data be gathered during the observation (video, audio, checklist, verbatim notes)?

3. What other information will help the observer to understand the lesson being taught?

Appendix 7.2—Verbatim Notes

Teacher:

    Class grade and subject:

Times for each lesson segment recorded:

Observer is watching for (wording of questions as higher- or lower-level ones; student feedback given; clarity of management statements; clarity of material presented; clarity of student tasks; statements and questions of students to the teacher; other):

Write exactly what the teacher or student says for the topic of observation for the lesson. Show and discuss the statements/questions with the teacher in the postconference.

Postconference questions to discuss with the teacher:

1. Were you aware that you started each question with _____?
2. Why did you phrase your positive feedback the way you did?
3. Why are students asking _____ multiple times?
4. How could you clarify instructions and directions for the students? Would visuals help?
5. With regard to statements about students' behaviors: do your statements help students to improve their behavior?

Appendix 7.3—Observation Postconference Template

1. Get teacher feedback, in general.

- How do you think the lesson went?
- Was the standard addressed as planned?
- Did you meet your planned teacher goal(s)?

2. Look at data gathered.

- Watch the video of the lesson or listen to the audio recording.
- Read the observer's verbatim notes.
- Review the observer's notes of teacher movement, student interaction, wait time, or other behavior that was observed.

3. Discuss and make conclusions from data.

- Is an intervention needed for the teacher (observing another teacher, reading about the issue, being observed by a mentor or colleague)?

4. Discussion of next steps of observation/supervision

- What questions does the teacher have about observations/supervisions?
- What questions does the teacher have, in general, about teaching and/or the final evaluation?

Appendix 7.4—First Classroom Walk-Through Checklist

1. The classroom desk/table arrangements are such that students have clear walkways to get to and from their seats.   _____ no _____ yes

Comment:

2. When the teacher is presenting, all students can face the front.   _____ no _____ yes

Comment:

3. There is a classroom management plan posted with rules, consequences, and positive reinforcements.   _____ no _____ yes

Comment:

4. School emergency procedures and other necessary guidelines are posted.   _____ no _____ yes

Comment:

5. The bulletin boards are covered and/or created with appropriate material.   _____ no _____ yes

Comment:

6. Evidence (visuals) of daily procedures and routines are posted.   _____ no _____ yes

Comment:

7. Materials and resources are organized (on shelves, in tubs, etc.)   _____ no _____ yes

Comment:

8. The learning targets and standards for learning are posted appropriately.   _____ no   _____ yes

Comment:

9. A daily schedule or list of what will be done is posted in the same spot every day for students.   _____ no   _____ yes

Comment:

Appendix 7.5—The Walk-Through Observation

Teacher:
Date and Time:
Grade/Subject:

1. Where is the teacher and what is he/she doing?

2. Where are the students and what are they doing?

3. Are visuals in use and can all students see them? (May check for specifics, such as a place for homework assignments posted.)

4. Is the classroom clean and organized?

5. What other areas will be observed? (For example, use of technology? Evidence of positive class climate?)

Appendix 8.1—Panel Discussion on Earning a Master's Degree

Arrangements: Ask for volunteers (4–6) who have recently completed a master's degree and who would be interested in sharing their experience. Allow at least an hour for the panel discussion, inviting all who are interested, but especially the new hires. Use the following questions to begin the discussion:

1. Describe where and when you earned your master's degree and why you chose that institution or program (online versus on campus, length of time to finish, cohort group or not, cost of program).
2. Which field is your master's degree in and why did you choose that area?
3. What was a typical class like in your program?
4. How much time outside of class was needed to complete work? How much research and writing were required?
5. What was the best part of the master's program you chose? What did you enjoy the most?
6. What were some of the challenges of the program you choose?
7. What is your best advice to those pursuing a master's degree now?

Facilitator's role:

1. Keep discussion on track.
2. May have an administrator or human resources staff member present to discuss specifics of tuition reimbursement offered, pay raise associated with the master's, and other details.

Appendix 9.1—Teachers' Needs and Wishes

Please rate the following on a scale of 1 to 5, where 1 indicates no need and 5 indicates high need.

1. Additional basic school supplies for students—pencils, paper, whiteboard markers   ____

2. More access to a copying machine and paper   ____

3. A cleaner classroom / more custodial help in my classroom   ____

4. More help from the administrative team with student behavioral issues   ____

5. More secretarial-type help (with reports, grade/data entry, copying)   ____

6. More training on our system's online resources (grade entry, website development, homework hotline)   ____

7. Updated technology/computers/student laptops   ____

8. More planned meeting time for small groups to work on planning, assessment, curricular issues, and individual student issues   ____

9. More assistance from special education teachers   ____

Now, please answer each question as specifically as possible.

1. What do you need to be a more effective teacher in your classroom?

2. If you could turn your job into your dream job, what would be on your wish list to make it your dream job? What would be on your wish list for the entire school to be the dream school as a workplace?

Appendix 9.2—Parent Satisfaction Survey

Please rate each of the following on a scale of 1 to 5, where 1 indicates no agreement and 5 indicates complete agreement.

1. I feel welcomed when I enter the school. ____

2. The school has a safe, orderly environment. ____

3. My student's teachers communicate with me about my student's achievement and behavior as needed. ____

4. My student's teachers inform me about what is taught, ongoing events, and testing. ____

5. I attend school events. ____

6. There are enough opportunities for me to meet and talk with my student's teachers. ____

Now, please answer each question.

1. List a change you would like to see at the school and why you feel that change has merit.

2. List a strength of the school and why that strength is important to you.

3. Complete this sentence: If I were a teacher at this school, I would like to . . .

Appendix 9.3—Survey of School Climate for Teachers

For each of the following, rate your agreement or disagreement with the statement. A number 1 indicates complete disagreement, and a number 5 indicates complete agreement.

1. When I was a new hire, I found the orientation sessions to be very useful. ____

2. When I was a new hire, the mentoring program provided much support. ____

3. As a new hire, I found the ongoing seminars just for new teacher were very helpful and supportive. ____

4. As a teacher with several years of experience, I find our school's culture to be very positive and supportive overall. ____

5. Our school is supportive with regard to the ongoing professional needs of teachers. ____

6. Our school has a comprehensive plan for student behavior and teachers are supported by the school's administrators with regard to student behavior. ____

7. School administrators have professional conversations with teachers. ____

8. School administrators have knowledge of teachers' strengths and apply that knowledge to plan schedules, getting teachers where they can best use their skills. ____

9. Teachers understand the curriculum to be taught and are given   _____
worthwhile training on curricular changes.

10. I have sufficient resources and supplies to do my job.   _____

11. I have sufficient technology to do my job.   _____

12. My classroom is kept clean and has a comfortable temperature.   _____

Appendix 9.4—Four-Step Approach for Classroom Management

This can be used to guide teachers who need help with management, as well as to evaluate the management of a teacher's classroom.

STEP 1: USE OF CLASSROOM SPACE AND ORGANIZATION OF THE ROOM

How the room is arranged is critically important. Is there a clear way to get to the seats in the room? Are all students able to see the screen or boards when the teacher presents? While tables and groups of desk are needed for activities, chairs should all face the front to start a school year and a school day. Seating arrangements do not have to be rows, but students need to face the front, as facing each other leads to immediate talking. Can the teacher circulate in the room?

STEP 2: PROCEDURES AND ROUTINES

What are the procedures for each activity of a class? The procedures should be made visual—a PowerPoint for high school students, posters for young students. The procedures include how to enter the room, leave the room, request help, get materials, participate in an activity, and so forth. The procedures must be taught and reinforced throughout the year. Procedures become positive routines.

STEP 3: THE CLASSROOM MANAGEMENT PLAN

The rules for classroom behaviors must be posted. Four or five behavioral rules cover the necessary behaviors. Examples include:

- Keep hands, feet, and objects to yourself.
- Follow all classroom procedures.
- No loud or rude talking.

Rules may be called guidelines, but must have consequences and positive reinforcements or supportive actions. The consequences in a classroom must fall under the parameters of the school's discipline policy, and the school must have a policy to support teachers' management plans. The management plan must be posted, sent home to parents, and in the principal's files (electronic or paper). Administrators may provide a template to each teacher for their management plan.

STEP 4: ENGAGED TEACHING MUST BE PLANNED AND IN PLACE

Teachers plan for on-task behavior in lesson plans. For each lesson segment, what is the teacher's role and what are students to be doing?

Administrators should devote time in every back-to-school orientation for the discussion and improvement of classroom management issues and student discipline. Additionally, walk-through classroom observations should always include checking for the classroom management poster and other posted procedures.

Appendix 9.5—A Four-Step Instructional Plan

STEP 1: FOCUS

- The focus starts lesson planning. The focus is generally built from a standard.
- Consider the teacher's goal(s) for the lesson.
- Be able to list the student outcome/objective of the lesson.
- Plan for an interesting, engaging hook for the lesson. A review or explanation of relevance or rationale will focus students.

STEP 2: PRESENTATION OF NEW MATERIAL

- Teachers should plan their instruction with action verbs—"reads," "models," "demonstrates," "explains."
- Teachers should always have visuals to guide learning.

STEP 3: APPLICATION OF MATERIAL

- Discussions, paired activities, group work, problem solving, writing, and editing are all applications.
- Applications keep students actively engaged in learning. (Evaluate by observing for students asking and answering questions, writing, researching, and participating in activities.)

STEP 4: REVIEW/CONCLUSION/ASSESSMENT

- Teachers summarize work; students summarize their learning verbally or in writing.
- Did the students meet or master objectives? How does the teacher know?

Appendix 9.6—Sample Quick Teacher Survey

Please rate the following on a scale of 1 to 5, where 1 indicates complete disagreement and 5 indicates complete agreement.

1. Homecoming week went very smoothly this year.   _____

2. Having all classes meet, but for a shortened period, worked well   _____
for the early dismissal on Friday.

3. There were limited problems and issues with the parade.   _____

4. The football game had few, or limited, problems.   _____

5. Homecoming week did not take away too much instructional   _____
time.

6. Teachers' duties at the homecoming events are about right in   _____
terms of time and work required.

7. Homecoming is scheduled at a good time in the semester.   _____

Now, please answer each question.

1. If you gave #7 a low rating, what would be your suggestion for a better time?

2. What do you recommend for the improvement of homecoming next year?

3. Are there other issues associated with homecoming and the week's activities that need addressing?

Appendix 10.1—Stress Management Survey

For each of the following, rate the level of stress you feel about the topic, on a scale of 1 to 10. Number 1 indicates no stress and 5 indicates significant stress.

1. Student behavior in my classes causes stress. _____

2. Students' emotional and home issues cause my stress. _____

3. Too many students in my class(es) is a stressor. _____

4. The mandated curriculum is a stressor. _____

5. Standardized testing is a stressor. _____

6. The low level of student achievement is a stressor. _____

7. The lack of an overall discipline plan in my school is a stressor. _____

8. Lack of parental support is a stressor in my job. _____

9. Lack of specific administrative support for my work is a stressor. _____

10. Teaching students who lack the academic background is a stressor. _____

11. Not having time for lunch and a break is a stressor. _____

12. Nonsupportive colleagues are a cause of stress. _____

13. Too much gossip and complaining in the school causes stress. _____

14. Salary and money management are stressors for me. _____

15. Time management is a stressful issue for me. _____

Now, for each issue that was marked with score of 8, 9, or 10: What intervention, training, or suggestion do YOU have as a possible course of action for improvement of the issue? List all that apply.

Appendix 10.2—Time Management Activities

TASK #1

Draw a big circle on a blank sheet of paper. The circle represents the twenty-four hours in a one day. Divide the circle, as a pie chart would be divided, with how you spend your day. For example, if you sleep six hours a night, that's 25 percent of your circle. Be honest.

- Consider your total hours at work. What percentage of your day is that?
- How long is your commute?
- How much time do you spend on schoolwork outside of the building?
- How much time is spent with your family?
- How much time is spent on housework, lawn work, or other home activities?
- How much free time do you have?
- How much time is spent watching TV or using social media?
- How much time is spent on exercise, meditation, or relaxation?

TASK #2

Study the circle you just created. Draw a second big circle on a sheet of paper. This time, divide the circle as a pie chart with the divisions you WANT to see in your day. How can you get your day to look more like the second circle? This is the biggest challenge of time management—eliminating some things so that you have the time to do what you consider more important. You have to decide and you can't do everything. You only have twenty-four hours in each day.

TASK #3 (MAY BE DONE BEFORE TASKS 1 AND 2)

- Choose a typical workday and list what you do from the time you wake up until you go to bed, with the amount of time for each thing on the list. Is there balance in your day?
- Choose a typical weekend day and repeat the activity.
- Study the two lists and ask yourself, "Is this how I want to spend my days?" If not, what can you change?

References

Acheson, K. A., & Gall, M. D. (2003). *Clinical supervision and teacher development: Preservice and inservice applications*. New York: John Wiley & Sons.

American Association for Employment in Education. (2015). *Job search handbook for educators*. Columbus, OH: American Association for Employment in Education.

Barker, K. (2015). The truth about millennial teachers. *ASCD Education Update*, 57(10), 7.

Barth, R. S. (2001). Teacher leader. *Phi Delta Kappan*, 82(6), 443–49.

Bond, N. (2011). Preparing preservice teachers to become teacher leaders. *Educational Forum*, 75(4), 280–97.

Bond, N. (2015). Introduction. In N. Bond (Ed.), *The power of teacher leaders* (pp. 1–3). New York: Routledge.

Bond, N. (2015). Teacher leaders as professional developers. In N. Bond (Ed.), *The power of teacher leaders* (pp. 57–69). New York: Routledge.

Boreen, J., Johnson, M. K., Niday, D., & Potts, J. (2009). *Mentoring beginning teachers: Guiding, reflecting, coaching*. (2nd ed.). Portland, ME: Stenhouse.

Borman, G. D., & Dowling, N. M. (2008). Teacher attrition and retention: A meta-analytic and narrative review of the research. *Review of Educational Research*, 78(3), 367–409.

Brill, S., & McCartney, A. (2008). Stopping the revolving door: Increasing teacher retention. *Politics & Policy*, 36(5), 750–74.

Brown, E. (Jan. 25, 2016). Sometimes, teacher turnover is a good thing, study finds. *The Washington Post*. Retrieved from https://www.washingtonpost.com/local/education/sometimes-teacher-turnover-is-a-good-thing-study-finds/2016/01/24/cb13cd14-c29f-11e5-8965-0607e0e265ce_story.html.

Canter, L., & Canter, M. (1993). *Succeeding with difficult students*. Bloomington, IN: Solution Tree.

Clement, M. C. (2012). Hiring the best. *Principal*, 92(1), 40–41.

Clement, M. C. (2015). *10 steps for hiring effective teachers*. Thousand Oaks, CA: Corwin.

Clement, M. C., & Wilkins, E. A. (2011). *The induction connection: Facilitating new teacher success*. Indianapolis: Kappa Delta Pi.

Danielson, C., & McGreal, T. L. (2000). *Teacher evaluation*. Alexandria, VA: Association for Supervision and Curriculum Development.

Darling-Hammond, L. (2003). Keeping good teachers: Why it matters, what leaders can do. *Educational Leadership*, 60(8), 6–13.

DeAngelis, K. J., & Presley, J. B., (2011). Toward a more nuanced understanding of new teacher attrition. *Education and Urban Society*, 43(5), 598–626.

Deems, R. S. (1994). *Interviewing: More than a gut feeling*. Des Moines, IA: American Media Publishing.

DiPaola, M. F., & Hoy, W. K. (2008). *Principals improving instruction: Supervision, evaluation, and professional development.* Boston: Pearson.

Espinoza, C., Ukleja, M., & Rusch, C. (2010). *Managing the Millennials.* Hoboken, NJ: John Wiley & Sons.

Farber, K. (2010). *Why great teachers quit: And how we might stop the exodus.* Thousand Oaks, CA: Corwin.

Fitzwater, T. L. (2000). *Behavior-based interviewing: Selecting the right person for the job.* Boston: Thomson.

Glickman, C. D., Gordon, S. P., & Ross-Gordon, J. M. (2001). *Supervision and instructional leadership: A developmental approach.* Boston: Allyn and Bacon.

Green, E., & Knight, H. (2015). S. F. teachers get help living in city under ambitious plan. Retrieved from http://www.sfgate.com/bayarea/article/Mayor-and-SFUSD-have-a-plan-to-help-teachers-keep-6583001.php.

Goddard, R., O'Brien, & Goddard, M. (2006). *Work environment predictors of beginning teacher burnout. British Educational Research Journal*, 32(6), 857–74.

Gruenert, S., & Whitaker, T. (2015). School culture rewired: How to define, assess, and transform it. Alexandria, VA: ASCD.

Hancock, C. B., & Scherff, L. (2010). Who will stay and who will leave? Predicting secondary English teacher attrition risk. *Journal of Teacher Education*, 61(4), 328–38.

Hargreaves, A. (2015). Foreword. In N. Bond (Ed.), *The power of teacher leaders* (pp. xiv–xv). New York: Routledge.

Henry, G. T., Bastian, K. C., & Fortner, C. K. (2011). Stayers and leavers: Early-career teacher effectiveness and attrition. *Educational Researcher*, 40(6), 271–80.

Hill, J. (2004). Five years later. *Journal of Education*, 185(1), 77–81. Retrieved from http://eds.a.ebscohost.com.

Howe, N., & Strauss, W. (2008). *Millennials and k–12 schools: Educational strategies for a new generation.* Great Falls, VA: Life Course Associates.

Ingersoll, R., Merrill, L., & Stuckey, D. (2014). *Seven trends: The transformation of the teaching force*, updated April 2014. CPRE Report (#RR-80). Philadelphia: Consortium for Policy Research in Education, University of Pennsylvania.

Inman, D., & Marlow, L. (2004). Teacher retention: Why do beginning teachers remain in the profession? *Education*, 124(4), 605–14.

Kessler, R. (2006). *Competency-based interviews.* Franklin Lakes, NJ: Career Press.

Levine, A., & Dean, D. R. (2012). *Generation on a tightrope: A portrait of today's college student.* San Francisco: Jossey-Bass.

Lewis, K. R. (Oct. 1, 2015). Nationwide's unusual practice of on-the-spot hiring. *Fortune.* Retrieved from http://fortune.com/2015/10/01/nationwides-on-the-spot-hiring.

Lieberman, A., & Wood, D. R. (2002). The National Writing Project. *Educational Leadership*, 59(6), 40–43.

Marzano (2012)

McEwan, E. K. (2002). *10 Traits of highly effective teachers: How to hire, coach, and mentor successful teachers.* Thousand Oaks, CA: Corwin.

Moore Johnson, S., & The Project on the Next Generation of Teachers. (2004). *Finders and keepers: Helping new teachers survive and thrive in our schools.* San Francisco: Jossey-Bass.

Murray, M. (1991). *Beyond the myths and magic of mentoring.* San Francisco: Jossey-Bass.

Nolan, J. F., & Hoover, L. A. (2011). *Teacher supervision and evaluation: Theory into practice.* Hoboken, NJ: John Wiley & Sons.

Owings, W. A., & Kaplan, L. S. (Spring 2008). Research on effective schools correlates: A summary and applications for public schools. *Journal for Effective Schools*, 7(1), 19–42.

Pollack, L. (2014). *Becoming the boss: New rules for the next generation of leaders.* New York: HarperCollins.

Portner, H. (2008). *Mentoring new teachers.* Thousand Oaks, CA: Corwin.

Rebore, R. W., & Walmsley, A. L. E. (2010). *Recruiting and retaining Generation Y teachers.* Thousand Oaks, CA: Corwin.

Richin, R., Banyon, R., Stein, R. P., & Banyon, F. (2003). *Induction: Connecting teacher recruitment to retention.* Thousand Oaks, CA: Corwin.

Rinke, C. R. (2014). *Why half of teachers leave the classroom: Understanding recruitment and retention in today's schools.* Lanham, MD: Rowman and Littlefield.

Rochkind, J., Ott, A., Immerwahr, J., Doble, J., & Johnson, J. (2007). *Lessons learned: New teachers talk about their jobs, challenges, and long-range plans.* A Report from the National Comprehensive Center for Teacher Quality and Public Agenda. Retrieved from www.publicagenda.org.

Scherer, M. (2012). The challenges of supporting new teachers. *Educational Leadership, 69*(8), 18–23.

Sclafani, S. K. (2015). Singapore chooses teachers carefully. *Phi Delta Kappan, 97*(3), 8–13.

Smith, T. M., & Ingersoll, R. M. (2004). What are the effects of induction and mentoring on beginning teacher turnover? *American Educational Research Journal, 41*(3), 681–714.

Steffy, B. E., Wolfe, M. P., Pasch, S. H., & Enz, B. J. (2000). *Life cycle of the career teacher.* Thousand Oaks, CA: Corwin.

Stronge, J. H. (2010). *Evaluating what good teachers do.* Larchmont, NY: Eye on Education.

Stronge, J. H., Tucker, P. D., & Hindman, J. L. (2004). *Handbook for qualities of effective teachers.* Alexandria, VA: ASCD.

Sujansky, J. G., & Ferri-Reed, J. (2009). *Keeping the Millennials.* Hoboken, NJ: John Wiley & Sons.

Sweeny, B. (2008). *Leading the teacher induction and mentoring program.* Thousand Oaks, CA: Corwin Press.

Trachtman, R., & Cooper, B. S. (2010). Teaching principals to be master teachers, again. In S. Conley (Ed.), *Preparing and orienting tomorrow's school leaders: Growth and life cycle approaches* (pp. 41–63). Lanham, MD: Rowman & Littlefield.

Truebridge, S. (2016). Resilience: It begins with beliefs. *Kappa Delta Pi Record, 52*(1), 22–27.

Twenge, J. M. (2006). *Generation me.* New York: Free Press.

Walsh, J. A., & Sattes, B. D. (2015). *Questioning for classroom discussion: Purposeful speaking, engaged listening, deep thinking.* Alexandria, VA: ASCD.

Winans, D. (May, 2005). It's hard to stick around. *NEA Today, 23*(8), 41.

Wong, H. K., & Wong, R. T. (2009). *The first days of school: How to be an effective teacher.* Mountain View, CA: Harry K. Wong.

Wong, H. K., & Wong, R. T. (2012). *Developing and retaining effective teachers and principals.* Mountain View, CA: Harry K. Wong Publications. Retrieved from www.effectiveteaching.com.

Index

About the Author

Mary C. Clement has researched the hiring and induction of teachers for more than twenty years, and her work has resulted in twelve previous books and more than a hundred articles. She has presented her work at ASCD and NAESP conferences, as well as for Phi Delta Kappa and Kappa Delta Pi. In 2013 she received the STAR award from the American Association for Employment in Education (AAEE) for her contribution to the research on teacher hiring.

A former high school teacher, she directed the Beginning Teacher Program at Eastern Illinois University for six years, providing training to administrators on how to induct and retain new teachers. Clement is now a professor of teacher education at Berry College in north Georgia. She earned her doctorate from the University of Illinois at Urbana–Champaign.